Morning Sidekick
Journal

Conquer Your Mornings, Conquer Your Life.

Created with love by
Amir Atighehchi, Ari Banayan, & Mikey Ahdoot

Copyright ©2018 Every Damn Day, LLC

All rights reserved.

Published by Every Damn Day, LLC.

No part of this publication may be reproduced, or stored in a retrieval system, or transmitted in any form or by any means, electronic, mechanical, recording, photocopying, scanning or otherwise, without express written permission of the publisher.

For information about permission to reproduce elections from this book, email team@habitnest.com

Visit our website at www.HabitNest.com

PUBLISHER'S DISCLAIMER

While the publisher and author have used their best efforts in preparing this book, they make no representations or warranties with respect to the accuracy or completeness of the contents of this book. The advice and strategies contained herein may not be suitable for your situation. You should consult with a professional where appropriate. Neither the publisher nor the author shall be liable for any loss of profit or any other commercial damages, including but not limited to special, incidental, consequential, or other damages.

The company, product, and service names used in this book are for identification purposes only. All trademarks and registered trademarks are the property of their respective owners.

ISBN (Sunrise Red): 9780692726716
ISBN (Beige): 9780998656137

FOURTH EDITION

Table of Contents

1   The "Why"
- Our Mission
- Understanding Your Why

9   The "What"
- The Phases of Building a New Habit
- Daily Content
- Eat That Frog

21   The "How"
- Perfectionists, Tread Lightly
- When Should I Wake Up?
- Common Challenges
- Holding Yourself Accountable
- Morning Routine Suggestions
- Sample Journal Page
- A Simple Idea
- Commit

40   Phase I (Days 1-7)

58   Phase II (Days 8-21)

92   Phase III (Days 22-66)

189   Fin
- So… What Now?
- About The Authors
- What Habit Will You Conquer Next?
- Share The Love
- Content Index

The "Why"

Our Mission

The truth of the matter is most people need some form of guidance when it comes to personal development.

Because you bought this journal, you're probably someone who is generally into personal development. You're probably familiar with ordinary journals that promise to help you remain productive, create useful routines, etc.

Let's be real.

Most journals have the same jargon and setup on every single page, and after looking at a simple cloned page that you've seen for a week straight, you become desensitized.

This journal is a compilation of the best tips and strategies discovered by people who have truly mastered their mornings. We've dug through many 300 page books, podcasts, scientific studies behind willpower, cool products/apps/gadgets, and dissected successful leaders' strategies to find the golden nuggets of info and present them here.

The result is a journal bringing something new to the table. **Actionable tips** and **motivating content** are what we're all about.

Every day, for 66 days, we're going to give you the information, motivation and accountability you need to stay consistent in making significant strides towards your goal of bettering yourself.

Why 66 days? In a recent study on human behavior, researcher Phillippa Lally discovered that on average, it takes 66 days to form a habit. In reality, there is no exact, definite, magical moment. But from personal experience, 66 days is a long enough time to build the habit so strongly that you can tap into it at any future point in your life.

You are building a life-altering habit here that you can use at any moment in your future. The beauty about this is by diving head first into mastering your mornings, you'll immediately start seeing the benefits on day ONE.

<u>Our mission is to be your book-sized personal trainer for building this life-altering habit into your day to day life.</u>

The way you start your morning sets the tone for the rest of your day. Building a morning routine that sets you up for the perfect day is one of the big "secrets" everyone knows but for some reason can't pull off.

"I'm not a morning person… I sleep too late… Just 5 more minutes…" **BS.**

Excuses are the *enemy of success*. Excuses are the *enemy of change*. Excuses are the *enemy of your goals*. Today we stop making excuses, together.

In this moment, you're already doing something amazing. The fact that you're reading this means somewhere in you there is a burning desire to really add this habit and make it stick.

Let's make it stick and add value to our lives in an amazing, indescribable way.

Understanding Your Why

As humans, what sets us apart from other animals is our desire to be great as opposed to simply survive. We all have a vision of what our ideal life might look like.

The absolute most important aspect of changing your life for the better is… **Knowing your damn *Why*.**

The thing is, when we forget (and we forget quite often) the reason we're struggling to improve our lives, we tend to retreat to our habitual selves - to the person we were before we made the decision to change.

Having a clear understanding of your "why" (what you want to change and why you want to change it) is what pulls you through the tough times you will inevitably face when altering your habits.

Here are a few simple questions that **you should take your time to answer sincerely before moving on**.

These questions are aimed at getting to the root of what drives you, what gets you up every single morning.

The point of this is to guide you to make concrete decisions about how to set up your morning to fit the beautiful vision you have for your perfect life.

If you're going to even make an attempt at this, you better know why you're doing it in the first place.

Seriously. Take the time to define your dream life.

1. What would my life look like if I did a morning routine filled with incredible habits every single day for the next 30 days?

_____
_____
_____
_____
_____
_____

2. What sort of ripple effect would doing a morning routine have on other areas of my life? On other people's lives around me?

_____
_____
_____

_____

_____

_____

_____

3. What would my life look like if I do not do this? What would I be missing out on? How would missing those make me feel?

_____

_____

_____

_____

_____

_____

_____

4. What life goals do I consistently avoid making time for? Can I implement taking action on these goals into my morning routine?

_____

_____

_____

_____

_____

Bonus Question: What are the top hurdles I'm facing with getting to bed on time / mastering my mornings? What do I need to do to overcome these?

_____

_____

_____

_____

_____

_____

Bookmark this section and flip back here the next time you're struggling to stay consistent with this habit.

This section is your SOS Lifeline.

The "What"

Phases of Building a New Habit

The development of building a habit happens in stages. There's science behind all kinds of different theories about the stages that come along with altering habits, and here's what we found is the most accurate.

*Days 1-7, **Hell Week.***

...This is going to suck.
It's going to suck because you're rewiring a lifetime habit to be totally different. Expect HELL. You're going to wake up EXHAUSTED. You will NOT easily fall asleep, especially on nights 1 and 2.

This will all fade. Guaranteed. It will fade because you will train your body to jump out of bed when you need to wake up. You will train it to turn off the lights at a specific time & shut off notifications, no matter how hyper your brain is. It will be tough, though your brain will learn. Your body will learn.

But for your brain and body to adapt, you must take action. You must distrust the challenging thoughts your brain will naturally give and show it what you want it to adapt to.

Daily challenges will give you specific actions to stay focused on while affirmations will set the tone for the direction your life is headed in.

Days 8-21, Staying Consistent.

The good news is that after you've gotten through the first week, the process is a lot easier. You've now hopefully figured out a few approaches that work. Your brain is beginning to understand the changes you're making and the fact that the morning time is extremely useful. Your body is slowly growing accustomed to your new hours. You're seeing the benefits of getting up and starting your day with intention.

During this period, a kick of inspiration can make all the difference. Developing habits takes time and just because you've surpassed the most difficult phase doesn't mean you're off the hook. You'll be reading stories of successful people and their morning routines, getting daily challenges to keep you motivated, and learning some more expert strategies along the way to keep the learning process going.

Days 22 - 66, Hardwiring - Retaining Interest In Your Personal Improvement.

Once you've passed phase 2, you know for a fact that YOU CAN DO THIS. It's amazing. All it takes is just about a month to add the habit, but that doesn't mean that phase 3 isn't crucial, because it is.

To build a habit means to become mechanical in a certain way. Your mind and your body will be used to the morning hours, you'll know the benefits of having a morning routine, but you still need to reach the point where there's no thinking about it anymore.

During phase 3 you'll get really cool and interesting tools that you might find useful for mastering your mornings. We'll continue to provide you with stories of successful people for motivation, and we'll continue to sprinkle in affirmations along the way to keep your brain active in making your morning routine a part of your DNA.

*Days 66 and on, **Habit Mastery**.*

At this point you've built up the muscle memory for mastering your mornings that you can use for life. Even if you won't be waking up early and doing a morning routine every day — after building this skill once, you'll be able to pick it back up at any future point easily.

From here, tweaking and experimenting with your mornings is what it's all about. Try different habits. Try different orders. Test out different wakeup times and go to bed times. You'll eventually find a rhythm that works well. The best part is you'll be navigating this like a pro at this point.

Experimenting can be interesting and enlightening. Feel free to plug in new habits you want to add to your life - the mornings are an incredible time to do them.

The Daily Content

Every single piece of content you're getting is a product of countless hours of sweat and research done by our team to ensure we're doing our best to:

1. Light a fire in you to succeed in adding the habit.
2. Provide you with the necessary knowledge and information to make mastering your mornings simple and easy.
3. Make adding the habit fun and interesting.

Not only is every individual piece of content chosen amongst thousands of competing options, but as mentioned in the previous section, the order of the content has been creatively designed to get you through the struggles associated with the different stages of adding habits.

Here are the different types of content you can expect:

Pro-Tips

Pro-tips are the golden little nuggets of information you get to make implementing the habit on a day-to-day basis as simple and painless as possible. The point is to give you expert tips and hacks to get you going, and the variety and diversity of the different pro-tips will provide you with countless options for how to succeed in adding the habit.

Daily Challenges

The daily challenges you'll be receiving will be immensely important to your success in becoming a morning riser.

Why?

They each help target a different area of discipline that will help you force yourself to do what's right, especially when you *don't feel like it.*

By strengthening this willpower muscle inside you using small, very specific daily challenges, your self-discipline will grow more and more every single day. These daily challenges apply not just to conquering your mornings but to all other aspects of your life — from curbing negative habits and distractions to building other healthy habits as well.

Clips & Podcasts

There's nothing as motivating as simultaneously seeing the passion in someone's eyes, hearing the truth in someone's voice, and feeling the intensity of their struggle. Connecting with people who have sat in your shoes and crossed over to the light of mastering their mornings will give you clear reference points that you *can* succeed at this, just as others who have struggled have. Watching or listening to inspirational and informational content will serve as the informative reminder you need to get started and push through your normal, expected struggles until you've mastered this.

Success Stories

The reason we want to alter our habits is that we have an image of how much more incredibly wonderful our lives can be; how much better WE can be. When we hear stories about successful people who live their lives in accordance with the ways we want to change, it is motivating, inspiring, and gives us a high standard to live up to.

Successful people (whether physically, financially, emotionally, or spiritually successful) exhibit the same daily patterns, one of which is a well-thought out and well practiced morning routine. Getting bits and pieces of information about existing success stories will get you going on those days you don't feel you have it in you; those days where you just don't remember what you're aiming for anymore.

By having a successful icon's morning routine dissected you can also get ideas for how to improve your own mornings.

We all need motivation, and understanding what it is that creates success for others will not only motivate you, but it will be a constant reminder of what it takes to be great.

Affirmations

Affirmations and visualization are highly effective tools used by some of the most successful people to have ever lived. From athletes to actors to CEOs, affirmations are used to help channel positive energy towards goals and create an inevitable connection between your present self and the end goal you have in mind.

What Affirmations Really Do

1. Unconsciously tap into your creativity muscle to begin generating creative ways of reaching your goals.

2. Unconsciously program your brain to associate yourself with the end goal you have in mind, and prepares you to mentally sort out the steps necessary to get from where you are right now to your end goals.

3. Attract you to your goal by the simple act of envisioning yourself where you want to ultimately be.

4. Motivate you in the sense that it literally causes your brain to believe that you have within you the power, ability and capability to get exactly where you want in life.

So What Does It Mean To Use Affirmations?

Using affirmations is the act of repeating to yourself that you already are the person you want to be.

Envisioning that you can achieve your life goals, and you can be exactly the person you ideally envision yourself to be.

It is the repeating of idealistic situations you would like to see yourself in, except you say them in the present tense, as if they were true now.

While repeating these affirmations, you visualize yourself as this ideal person, in the ideal situation you want to see yourself in, which trains your brain to believe it is possible.

Eat That Frog 🐸
Knock Out Your Most Important Task of the Day.

Mark Twain once said that if the first thing you do each morning is to eat a LIVE frog you fill yourself with a sense of strength and certainty that you've conquered the most difficult task of your day.

This sense of accomplishment makes you feel incredibly capable in tackling any other difficult tasks you have.

Brian Tracy elaborates on this concept in his amazing book, Eat That Frog (productivity nerds - this book is for you).

For the purposes of this journal, your "frog" is your biggest, most important task of the day - the one you are most likely to procrastinate on if you don't do something about it early on.

Every day you need to decide what your "frog" is for the day, and do your best to tackle that frog in the early hours of the morning.

Seeing how much better your day gets by tackling your "frog" early is the easiest way to fall in love with the morning. It'll instantly improve your quality of life ten-fold.

Challenge yourself to begin with your largest, most difficult, yet most significant task first. Start it right away, with no breaks, and push through until you complete it before you jump to something else.

Treat this as a test. Think of this as a personal challenge. Beat your temptation to start your day with any easier task.

The world's greatest leaders are each people who jump directly into their life's greatest tasks. They discipline themselves to work laser-focused until those tasks are finished.

Our brains are wired mentally and emotionally in such a way that the act of completing a task floods our brains with happiness.

You chemically reward your brain when you complete any task. You become happier. You feel like a winner. The larger and more difficult/important your task, the larger the impact it will have on your brain.

You will feel more confident. Radiant. More powerful. And ready to conquer the world.

You will quite literally grow a positive, healthy addiction (habit) for your brain to jump into a difficult task and complete it.

You will consistently rush your brain with endorphins. You'll feel mental clarity, confidence, and completeness, daily.

The "How"

Perfectionists, Tread Lightly.
The Importance of Not Getting Caught Up With Having "The Perfect/Best" Morning.

Of course, ideally we want to structure our morning in a way that makes the rest of our day flawless. We'd all love to wake up at 5 A.M., eat breakfast, exercise, read, write and meditate all before 7 A.M. and still start the day hours before most people on the planet open their eyes.

But sometimes there's a problem with shooting for perfection from the very start.

Shooting for perfection before you even complete your first morning routine can prevent you from ever taking one step in the direction of your goal.

So often you see people getting caught up in finding the best way to start working out, the best diet to lose weight, the most up-to-date research on the amount of sleep you need to be getting to feel amazing throughout the day…but I'll let you in on a little secret.

There's one simple concept that shatters all the best research, tips and strategies you can look for (that you'll be getting through this journal).

Here it is… the best way to become a morning person and begin forming a great morning routine is….

You start doing SOMETHING.

You start taking SOME actions towards your goal.

You make SOME effort.

Don't let the desire to reach perfection - the possibility of mastering your morning in a complete and wholesome way, disallow you from making sure you make today's morning better than yesterday.

Don't waste your energy fantasizing and searching.

The best way to determine YOUR ideal morning routine is by trying JUST ONE THING.

Nobody ELSE can tell you how to structure your morning. All they can do is give you information.

It's up to you to try ONE suggestion, and move forward from that point. Because altering your habits is about investigating what does and doesn't work FOR YOU, not for anyone else.

You'll be getting all the information and motivation you need from us on a daily basis in the form of daily content.

You won't PERSONALLY think every piece of content is useful. You won't think every tip will be effective. You won't think every podcast is insightful. You won't think every affirmation is worthwhile.

But if you make an attempt to use every piece of content, you'll see results. Pinky promise. Disregard the upside you *expect* out of it before trying it — take action first.

Every little action you take propels a snowball effect that greatly impacts other areas of your life.

If you push yourself to do a morning routine for even three days, you're gifting yourself a positive chain of effects that will improve your daily energy, mental clarity, and ability to crush important tasks. This is the true end goal of doing a morning routine, and arguably, of the journal as a whole.

In turn, when you don't prioritize the importance of your mornings, each of these things get sacrificed. Building a consistent healthy morning routine is one of the most powerful tools you have to help you become the best version of yourself as quickly as possible.

Help your body actually experience this so it has a positive reference point instead of just reading words on this page. Break through every obstacle and excuse you may face to absolutely get to bed early tonight and spend 15 minutes tomorrow morning doing any sort of morning routine.

Success is all about taking small, consistent actions over time.

When Should I Wake Up?

YOU CAN HAVE AN AMAZING MORNING AT ANYTIME

A common misconception is mixing up "waking up early" with "doing a morning routine."

The most important aspect of this is actually doing a daily routine (i.e. reading, exercising, meditating, etc. even if it's only for 5 minutes).

On days that you do not do your outlined rituals in the morning, *still fill out the journal.* As long as they get done they should be considered completed.

By forcing yourself to take action that will improve your life in the mornings, you set that same tone for the rest of your day.

Whether you start your morning at 5 A.M. or 11 A.M. isn't nearly as important as completing your morning objectives.

Although waking up early can be peaceful, serene, and energizing, that is NOT the main goal of this habit. We will refer to it throughout the journal because it can be very useful, but keep in mind it's not the essential key — daily routines are.

Even if you wake up late, you can still do your routine as part of your day. The main goal here is to just be consistent with what you're doing on a daily basis.

You WILL have days where you're absolutely off, down, and don't feel like "the best version of yourself."

These are the **MOST IMPORTANT** days to force yourself to do your daily routine.

This will rewire your brain to understand that it does not matter how incredibly good, utterly bad, or absolutely average your day is going. You WILL get your life habits done regardless.

Think about it:

- You ONLY have something to gain by doing this.
- The world's leaders undoubtedly implement this habit, and they also deal with the ordinary daily struggles we're all faced with.
- You don't lose ANYTHING by trying.

There is no reason for you not to commit to this habit with your heart and soul.

...Just take the first step.

Common Challenges
Doing A Morning Routine When You Have A Significant Other

Waking up early and doing a morning routine when you a significant other can be a challenge. The best solution here is of course, to have your partner join you in making the change.

If your significant other is not interested in changing their morning routine, which is completely fair and reasonable, there are a couple of action steps you can take to minimize the obstacle of having a partner with a different morning schedule:

After you write down fill out the 'Why' section in this journal, go ahead and show it to your partner.

Explain to them how important making this change is to you, and that although you understand if they don't want to join you, you are fully committed to becoming an early riser with a well intentioned morning routine.

Tell them specifically that you would really appreciate if they helped to keep you motivated throughout the process and reminded you how important this goal is to you when you're feeling discouraged.

Basically, let them know how much you would appreciate your partner being a positive force in making this change! The more specific you are about things that they can do to help you, or NOT do that might hurt your chances of waking up early or doing your routine, the easier it will be for them to be that positive force you need.

Doing A Morning Routine When You Work At Night

First of all - if you're the type of warrior who bought this journal when you work into the night, you're awesome.

Secondly, we want to emphasize that waking up early is a relative concept.

The point of this journal and incorporating the habit of waking up early and doing a morning routine is to begin your day intentionally, and before you 'have to' start the day.

If I start my ordinary day at 7 a.m., then waking up 'early' means starting the day before 7 o'clock with enough time to do a morning routine that will set me up for the perfect day. The same applies if I start my day at 4 or 5 p.m.

Stay focused on being intentional about what you do when you get up, before the obligations of the day begin is the goal.

Doing A Morning Routine When You Have Kids

Many, many of the wonderful people who have had success with this journal have children.

The reason being that it feels really good to have some alone time in the morning before your kids are up. It allows you to feel in control of your day rather than being run by the day.

If you have children and you're making this effort of waking up early and doing a morning routine, there are a couple of things to keep in mind.

If you want to wake up early, it's very important to get to bed at a reasonable hour, especially if you have kids. Having a no negotiation lights out time for yourself (if possible) is vital.

Depending on how old your children are and what your morning routine consists of, you can incorporate them into parts of your morning routine in different ways.

Try to be creative with it! If your children are old enough, doing activities together to start the day will help them naturally understand how important it is to start the day intentionally and calmly before the madness of the day begins. Plus, its incredible quality time you spend together.

We've had many stories from customers who talk about how valuable it is to have some time alone in the morning without the kids.

We've also received stories from mothers who do their morning routine with their kids (things like stretching, meditating, reading), and they believe that both they, and the kids are very positively impacted working on their habits together.

If you put some thought into it, you WILL make it work. Use your 'Why' to guide your morning decision making.

Holding Yourself Accountable

Using The Journal

Each day after getting out of bed, **put your journal on your pillow.** This will create a very easy trigger to remind you to use your journal and plan your next morning the night after. If you choose not to, it will need to be a much more conscious decision of physically picking the journal up and setting it aside to avoid just ignoring it on your nightstand.

The journal itself is also designed to create an accountability loop. In the nighttimes you map out and write out your morning routine. And in the mornings, you plan out the rest of your day and your nights. This creates an engaging cycle of accountability for yourself.

Staying Consistent

One of the best ways to continue doing this habit is to build it alongside a friend who is also passionate about becoming the best version of herself. Having someone to talk to and brainstorm about your specific pain points makes a huge difference. Her support (and sometimes competitive kick) can serve as a nice backup too.

We created a Facebook group specifically to hold yourself accountable to using this journal, getting daily support, and for building habits in general. Our team is extremely active on there and responds to every single post. Join the Habit Nest accountability group here:
facebook.com/groups/habitnest

Getting To Bed On Time

A huge part of mastering Your mornings falls on getting to bed on time the night before. Let's be real. THIS IS REALLY HARD. So how do we do this?

By setting clear boundaries - you *MUST* clarify your "lights out" time. This is especially useful to jump-start this habit.

First determine your wake up time *(let's say 5 A.M.)*. Now subtract how many hours you want to sleep. *(let's assume 7 hours. So lights out time is 10 P.M.)*. **Boom** - rocket science, complete.

A hack to make this process easier: Automatic Text Reminders! Use this tool: www.IFTTT.com

Make an account, create a new recipe, set the **IF** statement to "Date & Time" and choose "every day of the week at.." Customize the reminder leading up to lights out time.

Set the **ACTION** to SMS, connect your phone, and customize the message. You can even set multiple reminders from this.

We suggest keeping these active for 1 week to help you start the habit. Consider disabling them afterwards as you can easily get desensitized to them after a while.

Addressing Hard Days Ahead

Important: **you do not need to finish this journal in 66 consecutive calendar days in order for it to be effective!**

In fact, practically every single person who has prepared a morning routine has failed to follow it at some point.

Instead of trying to gloss over this, we're choosing to take a more practical approach by preparing specifically for those days of failure that will most likely blindside you when you least expect it (i.e. when your motivation is high or something sneaks up on you).

There's two keys to using these struggle days in a way that will benefit you:

First, empathize with yourself in that situation. Don't just think about it, actually feel what you'd be experiencing (i.e. if you were very motivated and one day you slipped up). Put yourself in that headspace.

Second, write out what the most disciplined version of yourself would do in that state, post-failure. Some examples of what your most disciplined self might do:

- Remove all guilt as you realize it's useless. Instead, you immediately search for WHY this happened.

- You get genuinely excited to keep going because you realize that you love challenges - each one you surpass makes you a stronger person.

- This time, you're mentally equipped with all you need to not let this specific mistake happen again.

- You realize this is a completely normal part of the self-improvement process - you gather all your energy, recoup mentally, and attack your day regardless.

Now, for the first time you truly struggle - what would you tell yourself and what would your actions be?

_____
_____
_____
_____
_____
_____
_____
_____

You don't have to do this exactly when you face your first struggle point, but having this as a reference can be extremely useful.

Morning Routine Suggestions

Let's Get Focused

There isn't a right answer to exactly how you should set up your morning. The key is to have a very real understanding of what you want to get out of it.

Your morning routine should bring about a specific outcome in your life. For example, it could be to create energy and momentum for your day or to knock out 1-2 of your most important tasks early on.

To get full clarity on this, write out what you want out of your mornings below. What should they set your day up for?

_____

_____

_____

_____

Examples Of What You Can Do With Your Mornings

For every activity that you put in your mornings, ask if it'll bring about the outcome you identified above or not.

It's also completely okay to experiment here — you can test different activities in your mornings and will likely change these consistently as time goes on. Here are some popular choices:

- Exercise
- Meditate
- Read
- Write or journal
- Work on a side project
- Get work done that you otherwise have to do later
- Spend time with loved ones
- Eat a good breakfast
- Do some household chores
- Go for a walk and listen to a podcast

These are all typical examples of the ways "morning people" start their days. You can create a routine by choosing your favorite actions from the above or creating your own.

You can do whatever you want with your morning as long as its furthering your goals, your desires and your life in a way that will impact your future positively.

Most "morning people" (aka anybody who's simply built this habit) create their routine around this concept.

Sample Journal Page

DATE _____

Night 0
(Begin Nighttime Routine).

TONIGHT I'LL SLEEP AT: __11:30pm__ & TOMORROW I'LL WAKE UP AT: __6:30am__

✨ MAGICAL MOMENT(S) I EXPERIENCED TODAY:

Watching the sunrise on my morning run :)

Finally made progress on my side-business!

☀ MY MORNING RITUAL TOMORROW WILL BE: *Completed?*

1. 5 minutes of meditation ✓
2. Read 2 pages of "Think and Grow Rich" ✓
3. Affirmations ☐
4. Walk 2 blocks outside ☐
5. Plan out and strategize the rest of my day ☐

Day 1
(Begin Morning Routine).

LAST NIGHT I SLEPT AT: __12am__ & WOKE UP TODAY AT: __7am__

🦌 MY MOST IMPORTANT TASK FOR TODAY IS:

Begin designing the app for my new startup

⊕ ONE WAY I CAN IMPROVE LIFE BY 1% IS:

Less Facebook / Instagram in the mornings

🧘 TOP TWO DISTRACTIONS TO MINIMIZE TONIGHT (BEFORE BED):

1. Watching YouTube in bed (limit: 15mins)
2. Watching the news (limit: 15mins)

A Simple Idea

We hope that after reading the introductory pages, you're motivated and ready to tackle tomorrow morning with every ounce of energy you have.

We'll leave you to it with one simple idea.

Tomorrow, you will be exactly who you are **today**.

The rest of your life is a future projection of who you are today.

If you **change** today, tomorrow will be **different**.

If you **don't change** today, the rest of your life is **predetermined**.

Commit.

No matter what happens tomorrow...

*whether I am exhausted
or have the **worst** day of my life...*

*...whether I win the lottery
or have the **best** day of my life...*

*I **will** do my morning
routine for the next week.*

*My word is like **gold**.*

*I will do whatever it takes
to make this happen.*

I **will** do my morning routine this week (circle one):

(On Weekdays Only)   (Every Damn Day)

_____   _____
Signature   Date

PHASE 1

DAYS 1-7

Phase 1	Phase 2	Phase 3
Days 01-07	Days 08-21	Days 22-66+
Hell Week.	Staying Consistent.	Rewiring Your Brain.

Phase 1: Hell Week

When beginning a new habit, what's really important is getting to the point where you start to see the benefits you expect. It isn't going to be easy to start. You need to believe in yourself and take at least one concrete step in the direction of your goal every single day during this phase because it's really easy to lose hope right off the bat.

Make use of every tip, every affirmation, and all the motivation you're getting to make it as easy as possible to take just one action towards your goal every day. Remember, we want to get to the point where we see benefits, and from that point on, self-motivation to re-acquire those benefits comes into play and smooths out the process.

Let's do this.

(Phase 1 Progress).

Day 1: **Pro-Tip**

Your morning ritual starts the night before.

Your nighttime ritual before each morning is very powerful. If your nighttimes are off, then your mornings will inevitably suffer.

All the extra decision-making you usually do in the morning can be done the night before. You don't want to become fatigued by small decisions before the day even starts.

One of the most useful nighttime rituals is preparing for your morning the night before. By removing any extra decisions from your morning, you will be able to wake up with full mental clarity and fly.

Each night, complete the following before going to bed:
1. Picking out your clothes
2. Choosing what you want to eat for breakfast
3. Getting your bag(s) together
4. The first task or ritual you will knock out when your day begins - this should be a task that you absolutely have to get done without question

"Lose an hour in the morning, and you will be all day hunting for it."
- Richard Whately

Night 0

(Begin Nighttime Routine).

DATE _____

(Write your predicted times).
TONIGHT I'LL SLEEP AT: _____ & TOMORROW I'LL WAKE UP AT: _____

MAGICAL MOMENT(S) I EXPERIENCED TODAY:
_____
_____

MY MORNING RITUAL TOMORROW WILL BE: *Completed?*

1. _____ ☐
2. _____ ☐
3. _____ ☐
4. _____ ☐
5. _____ ☐

Day 1

(Begin Morning Routine).

(Write the actual times).
LAST NIGHT I SLEPT AT: _____ & WOKE UP TODAY AT: _____

(Check these off in the morning!)

MY MOST IMPORTANT TASK FOR TODAY IS:
_____

ONE WAY I CAN IMPROVE LIFE BY 1% IS:
_____
_____

TOP TWO DISTRACTIONS TO MINIMIZE TONIGHT (BEFORE BED):

1. _____
2. _____

Day 2: **Daily Challenge**

<u>*Challenge: Use off days to rewire your brain by doing your habit when you LEAST "feel" like it.*</u>

The next time you wake up feeling tired or stressed is when it's MOST important to wake up and start the day out the way you planned it. This tells your brain: "This is happening. Nothing can get in my way. I'm unstoppable."

<u>*Newsflash*</u>: Your morning routine doesn't have to be "the best that it can be." Not even close.

You're going to have days where you feel OFF. The importance is actually doing it anyways. **No more excuses, just start your routine (even if it's done <u>horribly</u>).** *The goal: train your body to adopt the habit, even on off days.* <u>**This is one of the biggest keys to succeeding.**</u>

You'll *only* **FEEL** like doing your morning routine when you're in a positive mindset. **That's BS.**

Pick one option - you either get it done or you don't. *One or zero.* Use every ounce of energy you have to get it done. **Make today a <u>one</u>.** *Zero* isn't an option.

DATE _____

Night 1

TONIGHT I'LL SLEEP AT: _____ & TOMORROW I'LL WAKE UP AT: _____

🪄 MAGICAL MOMENT(S) I EXPERIENCED TODAY:

_____
_____

☀ MY MORNING RITUAL TOMORROW WILL BE: *Completed?*

(Make these SMALL! i.e. read 2 pages, not 10 pages).

1. _____ ☐
2. _____ ☐
3. _____ ☐
4. _____ ☐
5. _____ ☐

Day 2

LAST NIGHT I SLEPT AT: _____ & WOKE UP TODAY AT: _____

🐸 MY MOST IMPORTANT TASK FOR TODAY IS:

_____

⏲ ONE WAY I CAN IMPROVE LIFE BY 1% IS:

_____

(Reminder: this journal doesn't have to be completed in 66 calendar days! If you miss a day or more, resume when ready).

🧘 TOP TWO DISTRACTIONS TO MINIMIZE TONIGHT (BEFORE BED):

(Try setting a generous yet strict time limit for these).

1. _____
2. _____

Day 3: **Pro-Tip**

<u>Condition yourself week-by-week to wake up earlier</u>

Make the process of becoming an early riser with a morning routine a true transition. If you always wake up at 10 or 11am, it isn't too realistic to expect that you will immediately wake up at 5am the next day. Start off by improving your waking time by 15~30 minutes a day until you reach your goal. We would recommend even improving your wake up time by 15-30 minutes every **week**.

Small victories are one of the keys to success. This applies to anything in life, but can be used specifically for easing into altering your wakeup time.

It may feel less rewarding initially, but if you try to make a dramatic change all at once, chances are you'll hit a wall, ruin your workday on multiple occasions, and consequently become discouraged. Make your goals attainable without shocking your body and really try to condition yourself in a natural and holistic way.

"Opportunities are like sunrises. If you wait too long, you miss them."
- William Arthur Ward

Night 2

DATE: _____

TONIGHT I'LL SLEEP AT: _____ & TOMORROW I'LL WAKE UP AT: _____

✨ MAGICAL MOMENT(S) I EXPERIENCED TODAY:

_____
_____

(Bonus points if you actually FEEL the added happiness from these).

☀ MY MORNING RITUAL TOMORROW WILL BE:

Completed?

(By making these small, you're making it insanely easy to succeed).

1. _____ ☐
2. _____ ☐
3. _____ ☐
4. _____ ☐
5. _____ ☐

Day 3

LAST NIGHT I SLEPT AT: _____ & WOKE UP TODAY AT: _____

🐸 MY MOST IMPORTANT TASK FOR TODAY IS:

_____
_____

(This can be completed anytime, not just the mornings).

⬆ ONE WAY I CAN IMPROVE LIFE BY 1% IS:

_____
_____

🧘 TOP TWO DISTRACTIONS TO MINIMIZE TONIGHT (BEFORE BED):

1. _____
2. _____

Day 4: **Daily Challenge**

Challenge: Write down what factors have recently impeded you from successfully performing your morning routine.

Envision the most recent time you completely "failed" at your morning routine or had some other negative experience with it.

Now breathe…Everybody, and I mean everybody struggles with consistency. The truth is that imperfect days teach us the most about how to succeed.

Treat days you mess up as experiments. By consciously writing down what factors caused us to struggle, we can better prepare against them.

On days you aren't "perfect", try to answer these questions:

1. What was my thought process during the first decision I made that led me astray from having an even better day? What can I learn from this to apply moving forward?
2. In addition to the above, what are some additional "rules" you can set to prevent what caused this specific slip-up in the future?
3. What justification did you tell yourself to make it okay to slip up?

These mental insights can really act as secret weapons on days we struggle. We will all miss doing our habits. Let's make those days just as valuable as perfect days by treating them as learning experiences.

Night 3

DATE _____

TONIGHT I'LL SLEEP AT: _____ & TOMORROW I'LL WAKE UP AT: _____

🪄 MAGICAL MOMENT(S) I EXPERIENCED TODAY:

_____

_____

☀ MY MORNING RITUAL TOMORROW WILL BE:

Completed?

(Use your nights to keep yourself accountable in the mornings).

1. _____ ☐
2. _____ ☐
3. _____ ☐
4. _____ ☐
5. _____ ☐

Day 4

LAST NIGHT I SLEPT AT: _____ & WOKE UP TODAY AT: _____

🐸 MY MOST IMPORTANT TASK FOR TODAY IS:

_____

⊕ ONE WAY I CAN IMPROVE LIFE BY 1% IS:

_____

(GUILT is a discipline destroyer. Don't be perfect, be practical).

🧘 TOP TWO DISTRACTIONS TO MINIMIZE TONIGHT (BEFORE BED):

(Set an actual timer to track these. Apple's iOS 12 allows limit timers, as do all Androids).

1. _____
2. _____

Day 5: **Pro-Tip**

Find a morning accountability partner

Find another friend who is as ambitious and committed to bettering themselves as you are. Together, devise a scheme for holding each other accountable to waking up and beginning the day with a clear intention. Even just promising to text each other when it's time to rise and shine will do wonders.

1. Find someone as ambitious as you are that can serve as an accountability partner.
2. Select a goal wake-up time.
3. Pick a method of evidence.
   A. Send him/her a selfie of waking up.
   B. Text him/her when you're up.
   C. Call him/her when you're up.

Superhero Option: Determine what time you and your partner want to wake up. Only one of you sets an alarm so you know the other is counting on you to wake them up!

"I'm always craving that dreamy creative energy I can only get while the rest of the world is asleep." – Lindsay Champion

DATE _____

Night 4

TONIGHT I'LL SLEEP AT: _____ & TOMORROW I'LL WAKE UP AT: _____

🪄 **MAGICAL MOMENT(S) I EXPERIENCED TODAY:**

_____

_____

(These should be so easy to do it should feel almost like a joke to hit your minimums).

☀️ **MY MORNING RITUAL TOMORROW WILL BE:**   *Completed?*

1. _____ ☐
2. _____ ☐
3. _____ ☐
4. _____ ☐
5. _____ ☐

Day 5

LAST NIGHT I SLEPT AT: _____ & WOKE UP TODAY AT: _____

🐸 **MY MOST IMPORTANT TASK FOR TODAY IS:**

_____

(Starting your day for 5min with this = huge win).

⏱ **ONE WAY I CAN IMPROVE LIFE BY 1% IS:**

_____

(Note: These distractions are okay to have - but own them by being mindful of them).

🧘 **TOP TWO DISTRACTIONS TO MINIMIZE TONIGHT (BEFORE BED):**

1. _____
2. _____

Day 6: **Pro-Tip**

Some strategies for chronic snoozers.
Snoozing can be an incredibly difficult habit to break or overcome. Here are some tips that you can try (or combine for maximum effectiveness):

1. Make it a rule not to turn off your alarm until you've **stepped out of bed** and are standing up.

2. Learn exactly the right amount of sleep you need (hours wise) to have a fantastic day. You need to experiment with what that number is for you. Once you have it though, you should set your go to bed and wake up times based on that.

   Now when your alarm goes off, you can have *trust and respect* for it, based on the times you set. Even if you're tired in that moment, you'll know deep down that (if set correctly) you got the right amount of sleep and there's no value for you to sleep in.

3. Realize that it's **perfectly okay to be tired when you get** up in the morning. Instead, you can allow your body to wake up as you begin your day and morning routine. Remember, start moving!

"If you really think about it, hitting the snooze button in the morning doesn't even make sense. It's like saying, 'I hate getting up in the morning- so I do it over... and over... and over again.'" - Demetri Martin

DATE _____

Night 5

TONIGHT I'LL SLEEP AT: _____ & TOMORROW I'LL WAKE UP AT: _____

🪄 **MAGICAL MOMENT(S) I EXPERIENCED TODAY:**

_____

_____

☀️ **MY MORNING RITUAL TOMORROW WILL BE:**   *Completed?*

(Being consistent is about 1000x more important than how WELL you do these).

1. _____ ☐
2. _____ ☐
3. _____ ☐
4. _____ ☐
5. _____ ☐

Day 6

LAST NIGHT I SLEPT AT: _____ & WOKE UP TODAY AT: _____

🐎 **MY MOST IMPORTANT TASK FOR TODAY IS:**

_____

🎯 **ONE WAY I CAN IMPROVE LIFE BY 1% IS:**

_____

🧘 **TOP TWO DISTRACTIONS TO MINIMIZE TONIGHT (BEFORE BED):**

1. _____
2. _____

(Don't feel guilty if you don't hit these predictions. Instead, investigate WHY you didn't).

Phase 1 Complete!

Day 7: **Affirmations**

1. Find a quiet area where you can do this in private so you can be at ease. If you can't find a private space, say these in your head while pretending you're screaming them from a mountaintop.

2. Think of a time when you felt absolutely powerful - **when you felt on top of the world**. Tap into every emotion you had at that moment and get yourself into that state right now. How were you feeling then - Powerful? Unstoppable? Strong? Incredible!? Get into it now!!!!

3. Now feel your intensity grow tenfold! Say this with deep passion:

I will get out of bed as soon as my alarm goes off at ____ A.M. and begin the day with positivity and intention.

Like the most successful people around the world, I understand that to succeed, I must utilize my life every damn day to its full potential.

I can easily wake up early every day. I will make my days incredibly uplifting, energetic, and productive.

Repeat this **one more time.**

"It is well to be up before daybreak, for such habits contribute to health, wealth, and wisdom." - Aristotle

Pssssttt... We like rewarding people (like you) who TAKE ACTION and actually use this journal. Email us now at secret+morning@habitnest.com for a secret gift ;)

DATE _____

Night 6

TONIGHT I'LL SLEEP AT: _____ & TOMORROW I'LL WAKE UP AT: _____

🪄 MAGICAL MOMENT(S) I EXPERIENCED TODAY:

_____
_____

☀️ MY MORNING RITUAL TOMORROW WILL BE:

Completed?

1. _____ ☐
2. _____ ☐
3. _____ ☐
4. _____ ☐
5. _____ ☐

Day 7

LAST NIGHT I SLEPT AT: _____ & WOKE UP TODAY AT: _____

🐎 MY MOST IMPORTANT TASK FOR TODAY IS:

_____
_____

⬆️ ONE WAY I CAN IMPROVE LIFE BY 1% IS:

_____
_____

🧘 TOP TWO DISTRACTIONS TO MINIMIZE TONIGHT (BEFORE BED):

1. _____
2. _____

~~PHASE 1:~~ CONQUERED.

Phase 1 Recap: Days 1-7

1. What morning rituals do you want to continue doing?

_____
_____

2. What rituals were not useful for you that you'll cut?

_____
_____

3. What are some new rituals you want to experiment with?

_____
_____

4. If you continued this habit for another 2 weeks, what kind of person would you become?

_____
_____
_____

5. If you dropped this habit now, would it benefit your life in any way?

_____
_____
_____

PHASE 2
DAYS 8-21

 ~~Phase 1~~ | **Phase 2** | Phase 3

~~Days 01-07~~
~~Hell Week.~~ | **Days 08-21**
Staying Consistent. | Days 22-66+
Rewiring Your Brain.

Phase 2: Digging Deep - Staying Consistent

Congratulations, you've gotten through Phase 1 (Hell Week).

If you don't feel like you've made as much progress as you'd like, don't worry. One day and one victory at a time is the key.

Phase 2 is important because this is the point where we either feel like we've got it down, OR we feel hopeless that we'll never reach our goals. Either way, ignore what your mind says. If you feel like you've reached your goal, don't trust the feeling because now you need to STAY consistent.

If you feel hopeless, you won't feel hopeless forever as long as you continue to believe in yourself and make a real effort daily.

Note: this phase features a **new section** in place of distractions - **benefits**! These can help you stay consistent by seeing what you're GAINING from doing your routine daily.

One huge thing to watch out for: On days people miss routines, many people end up circling 0 benefits that day. This leads them to feeling like they scored a "0/6" that day and are naturally bad at this (which they're not, everybody misses days), and thus use it as a trigger to fall off the wagon. Be mindful of this on days you struggle and **stick with it!**

Commit.

*I KNOW this next phase
is going to be extremely hard.*

*I understand I may not
be perfect about it every day.*

*But I <u>will</u> put my heart, each day, into
conquering this life-changing goal.*

**If I miss a day,
I will pick back up.**

*Off days and missed days
will NEVER stop me.*

*In the long-run,
I will win.*

I <u>will</u> complete Phase 2 of this journal.

_____   _____
Signature   Date

Phase 1 Medal Earned!

Day 8: **Daily Challenge**

<u>Challenge: Pay attention to the mini decisions you make. Ask yourself, "If I made this choice EVERY DAY, would I be a lot closer to my goals, or a lot further?"</u>

<u>Newsflash</u>: **Your choices are 100 times more important than you think.** Every choice you make today is building up a habit for the rest of your life. Our brains learn from what we do repeatedly - the decision to oversleep is in reality 100x more powerful over time.

Taking one tiny action in a positive direction has the same effect. From little things, like waking up 5 minutes earlier — to big things like doing an important task first thing in the morning or pushing through that last rep of your workout when you have nothing left in the tank. This snowballs over time into the person you are becoming.

You can justify not doing your habit, but your mind and body grow accustomed to it. Creating excuses is a mental habit that can absolutely be rewired. Your brain only knows **what you do**. When you start the day with intention, your brain rewires itself. *All mini decisions build up to your habits.* **You** *are* **your mini-decisions.**

"Don't let the old you make your decisions. Today is the only day change exists. Change today and your entire life will be altered. Don't change today, and tomorrow will be exactly like today, forever." - Ari Banayan

Night 7

DATE: _____

TONIGHT I'LL SLEEP AT: _____ & TOMORROW I'LL WAKE UP AT: _____

🪄 MAGICAL MOMENT(S) I EXPERIENCED TODAY:

_____

_____

(Phase 2 is a great time to revisit your "Why" on page 5 again).

✓ BENEFITS I FELT TODAY (CIRCLE):

☺ Feel Happier | ≡ More Organized | ☀ Fuller Days | ✓ Increased Productivity | ♥ More Energized | 🧘 Reduced Stress

(Try combining a few simpler steps into one line, i.e. brush teeth + shower + bathroom).

☀ MY MORNING RITUAL TOMORROW WILL BE: *Completed?*

1. _____ ☐
2. _____ ☐
3. _____ ☐
4. _____ ☐
5. _____ ☐

Day 8

LAST NIGHT I SLEPT AT: _____ & WOKE UP TODAY AT: _____

🐸 MY MOST IMPORTANT TASK FOR TODAY IS:

_____

_____

⊕ ONE WAY I CAN IMPROVE LIFE BY 1% IS:

_____

Day 9: **Super Read**

Title: *The Miracle Morning*
Author: Hal Elrod

# of Amazon Reviews: 3,167
★★★★★ 4.7/5

The Miracle Morning is an incredible book about creating the best morning routine on the planet. Hal's life story is pretty amazing, having survived a car crash that left him dead for six minutes.

This book will help you jumpstart your mornings by implementing a morning routine called the Life S.A.V.E.R.S. Hal breaks down into specific actionable steps how to implement Silence (meditation), Affirmations, Visualization, Exercise, Reading, and Scribing (writing/journaling).

We could not recommend this book more highly as it has transformed how we master our mornings daily.

Where to get it: Search "Miracle Morning" on Amazon.

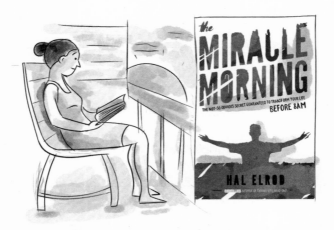

"The moment you accept responsibility for EVERYTHING in your life is the moment you can change ANYTHING in your life." - Hal Elrod

DATE _____

Night 8

TONIGHT I'LL SLEEP AT: _____ & TOMORROW I'LL WAKE UP AT: _____

🪄 **MAGICAL MOMENT(S) I EXPERIENCED TODAY:**

_____

_____

✓ **BENEFITS I FELT TODAY (CIRCLE):**

Feel Happier · More Organized · Fuller Days · Increased Productivity · More Energized · Reduced Stress

(If your weekdays/weekends fluctuate, feel free to create different routines & wake up times for each).

☀ **MY MORNING RITUAL TOMORROW WILL BE:**   *Completed?*

1. _____ ☐
2. _____ ☐
3. _____ ☐
4. _____ ☐
5. _____ ☐

Day 9

LAST NIGHT I SLEPT AT: _____ & WOKE UP TODAY AT: _____

🐸 **MY MOST IMPORTANT TASK FOR TODAY IS:**

_____

🧭 **ONE WAY I CAN IMPROVE LIFE BY 1% IS:**

_____

(Setting TINY, EASILY ACHIEVABLE daily goals is one of the greatest discipline hacks out there).

65

Day 10: **Pro-Tip**

Re-boot your sleep schedule.

If you are sleeping very late, chances are your brain is wired to get consistent dopamine rushes and immediate gratification that keep you awake.

That's okay, this is very common and easy to fix. <u>Take these steps</u>:

1. Set an alarm for 5 hours after your go-to-bed time. When your alarm goes off tomorrow, JUMP out of bed. Be OKAY with the tiredness — this will last a few hours and will fade.
2. Later that day, you will be tired once again. Use this to your advantage to fall asleep early tomorrow night. Do not nap.
3. Set a clear "lights out" time. When this time comes, shut off all electronics (airplane mode), lights, & distractions.
4. Two options: either read a book or listen to a podcast (download it so it's available offline, in airplane mode) until you fall asleep.

This is the quick, *one-time hack* to reboot your sleeping schedule to help you sleep earlier. If you've got sleeping early down, waking up early/doing a morning routine will follow.

"If you wake up and you're not looking forward to the day ahead, you need to re-evaluate your life." - Ari Banayan

DATE _____

Night 9

TONIGHT I'LL SLEEP AT: _____ & TOMORROW I'LL WAKE UP AT: _____

(For added accountability, put your journal on your pillow after each morning routine).

MAGICAL MOMENT(S) I EXPERIENCED TODAY:

_____

_____

BENEFITS I FELT TODAY (CIRCLE):

- Feel Happier
- More Organized
- Fuller Days
- Increased Productivity
- More Energized
- Reduced Stress

MY MORNING RITUAL TOMORROW WILL BE: *Completed?*

1. _____ ☐
2. _____ ☐
3. _____ ☐
4. _____ ☐
5. _____ ☐

Day 10

LAST NIGHT I SLEPT AT: _____ & WOKE UP TODAY AT: _____

(You don't always have to fill in 5 things here, it's up to you).

MY MOST IMPORTANT TASK FOR TODAY IS:

_____

ONE WAY I CAN IMPROVE LIFE BY 1% IS:

_____

Day 11: **Affirmations**

1. Find a quiet area where you can do this in private so you can be at ease. If you can't find a private space, say these in your head while pretending you're screaming them from a mountaintop.

2. Think of a time when you felt absolutely powerful - **when you felt on top of the world.** Tap into every emotion you had at that moment and get yourself into that state right now. How were you feeling then - Powerful? Unstoppable? Strong? Incredible!? Get into it now!!!!

3. Now feel your intensity grow tenfold! Say this with deep passion:

I have limitless drive and energy because I wake up at ____ A.M. Waking up early gives me the time to optimize my body and mind before the day starts. Starting the day while the rest of the world is still asleep fills me with incredible confidence, energy and enthusiasm! I am truly unstoppable!!

Repeat this **one more time.**

"When you arise in the morning, think of what a precious privilege it is to be alive - to breathe, to think, to enjoy, to love - then make that day count!" - *Steve Maraboli*

(Try experimenting with how many hours of sleep you actually need. Test a different number for 3 days straight starting today).

DATE _____

Night 10

TONIGHT I'LL SLEEP AT: _____ & TOMORROW I'LL WAKE UP AT: _____

🪄 MAGICAL MOMENT(S) I EXPERIENCED TODAY:

_____

_____

(Remember: it's normal to have off-days and miss these).

✓ BENEFITS I FELT TODAY (CIRCLE):

Feel Happier · More Organized · Fuller Days · Increased Productivity · More Energized · Reduced Stress

🌅 MY MORNING RITUAL TOMORROW WILL BE: *Completed?*

1. _____ ☐
2. _____ ☐
3. _____ ☐
4. _____ ☐
5. _____ ☐

(No guilt allowed for missing these! Only learning).

Day 11

☀️ LAST NIGHT I SLEPT AT: _____ & WOKE UP TODAY AT: _____

🐎 MY MOST IMPORTANT TASK FOR TODAY IS:

_____

🎯 ONE WAY I CAN IMPROVE LIFE BY 1% IS:

_____

Day 12: **Success Story**
Arianna Huffington: Founder of Huffington Post & Thrive Gobal

Arianna is a superwoman. Her story begins with her being sleep deprived and overworking to exhaustion - to the point that she *passed out on the table and broke her cheekbone*. She now makes it a priority to allow herself ample rest and recovery time, despite how hard she works.

In the morning, she avoids using her phone and instead jumps into exercise and meditation. She skips breakfast in place of coffee too.

One big takeaway from Arianna is how strongly she uses her nighttime routine to her advantage. By turning off all electronics and moving them out of the room, she allows herself to fully focus on sleep at night.

Oftentimes, one of the most rewarding obstacles to conquer is getting to bed on time and minimizing unnecessary distractions at night. Are there any changes you can make to your nighttime routine that would make a big impact on your mornings?

"When I'm tempted to skip my morning routine or another form of self-care, I remind myself that I can better serve the people I love and the projects I care about when I start with me." - Courtney Carver

DATE _____

🌙 **Night 11**

TONIGHT I'LL SLEEP AT: _____ & TOMORROW I'LL WAKE UP AT: _____

🪄 **MAGICAL MOMENT(S) I EXPERIENCED TODAY:**

_____
_____

✓ **BENEFITS I FELT TODAY (CIRCLE):**

😊	📋	🌅	⏱	⚡	🧘
Feel Happier	More Organized	Fuller Days	Increased Productivity	More Energized	Reduced Stress

(If it's helpful, you can write in the times you expect to do each of these as well).

☀ **MY MORNING RITUAL TOMORROW WILL BE:** *Completed?*

1. _____ ☐
2. _____ ☐
3. _____ ☐
4. _____ ☐
5. _____ ☐

☀ **Day 12**

LAST NIGHT I SLEPT AT: _____ & WOKE UP TODAY AT: _____

🐎 **MY MOST IMPORTANT TASK FOR TODAY IS:**

_____

🎯 **ONE WAY I CAN IMPROVE LIFE BY 1% IS:**

_____

(Follow the chain of effects that cause your off-days. Where did it all start from?).

Day 13: **Double Pro-Tip** 💡💡

Drink a glass of ice cold water right when you get up.

When you wake up after a night of sleep, your body is naturally dehydrated. Drinking water as soon as you wakeup provides your cells with much needed nourishment & energy. One glass of water will wake you up, instantly fire up your metabolism, flush out unnecessary toxins, fuel your brain and suppress your appetite.

1. Have a glass sitting next to your fridge for your morning water

Also, when you're groggy or tired, you need a shock to your system to really wake up. Loud music provides that shock to get your mind and body rolling.

2. Play your favorite upbeat, fast tempo music right when you wake up! Keep headphones by your bed so you can play them as loudly as you feel comfortable with (and that won't deafen you).

The best way to do this is to create a playlist with at least 10 different songs so you don't get desensitized to it at all.

Superhero Option: Another shock to your system that works well is doing 10-20 seconds of an exercise as soon as you get out of bed. You can try doing 10 jumping jacks or pushups and you'll instantly be more awake.

"The sun has not caught me in bed in fifty years." - Thomas Jefferson

(Important: the days you DON'T FEEL like doing these are the MOST IMPORTANT days to do them! It shows your brain that you're unstoppable).

DATE: _____

Night 12

TONIGHT I'LL SLEEP AT: _____ & TOMORROW I'LL WAKE UP AT: _____

🪄 MAGICAL MOMENT(S) I EXPERIENCED TODAY:

_____
_____

✓ BENEFITS I FELT TODAY (CIRCLE):

- 🙂 Feel Happier
- 📋 More Organized
- 🌅 Fuller Days
- ⏱ Increased Productivity
- ❤⚡ More Energized
- 🧘 Reduced Stress

(You can always surpass a small goal and feel even BETTER about yourself).

🌅 MY MORNING RITUAL TOMORROW WILL BE: *Completed?*

1. _____ ☐
2. _____ ☐
3. _____ ☐
4. _____ ☐
5. _____ ☐

☀ Day 13

LAST NIGHT I SLEPT AT: _____ & WOKE UP TODAY AT: _____

🐸 MY MOST IMPORTANT TASK FOR TODAY IS:

_____
_____

🎯 ONE WAY I CAN IMPROVE LIFE BY 1% IS:

_____
_____

Day 14: **Favorite Podcasts**

Sleep With Me Podcast.

iTunes Reviews: 5,440
★★★★★ 4.5

The "Sleep With Me" podcast is designed to put you to sleep. They do it with a bedtime story. Yes, you read it right, a bedtime story. Just get in bed, press play and drift off into dreamland. Their description is "A Lulling, Droning, Boring Bedtime Story to Distract Your Racing Mind." It is rated 5 stars and is definitely something to try.

You can get started by:

1. Find the podcast "Sleep With Me" and choose an episode to listen to.
2. Download the episode to your phone.
3. Go in airplane mode and play the episode.
4. Set your podcast player to automatically stop after the current episode finishes. You can do this on iOS by hitting the moon icon on the bottom of the podcast page (while an episode is playing) and selecting the time you want it to stop playing.

"Man should forget his anger before he lies down to sleep."
-Mohandas Gandhi

Night 13

(If meditation is part of your routine, consider using an app like Headspace or our Meditation Sidekick Journal to help grow it further).

DATE _____

TONIGHT I'LL SLEEP AT: _____ & TOMORROW I'LL WAKE UP AT: _____

MAGICAL MOMENT(S) I EXPERIENCED TODAY:

_____
_____

BENEFITS I FELT TODAY (CIRCLE):

Feel Happier | More Organized | Fuller Days | Increased Productivity | More Energized | Reduced Stress

MY MORNING RITUAL TOMORROW WILL BE:

Completed?

1. _____ ☐
2. _____ ☐
3. _____ ☐
4. _____ ☐
5. _____ ☐

Day 14

LAST NIGHT I SLEPT AT: _____ & WOKE UP TODAY AT: _____

MY MOST IMPORTANT TASK FOR TODAY IS:

_____

ONE WAY I CAN IMPROVE LIFE BY 1% IS:

_____

Day 15: **Daily Challenge**

<u>**Challenge:** Determine an activity that'll have you excited about waking up to start the day and insert it into your routine.</u>

If you wake up and dread whatever is ahead of you in the day, it doesn't matter what time you wake up - you'll hate it. When you wake up without excitement, it is hard to even get out of bed.

But if you figure out how to make your mornings exciting – if you wake up and you're like, "I can't wait to get up. This day is going to be awesome. I'm going to do SO MUCH this morning and set an example for not just the rest of my day but the rest of my week and life!" you put yourself in a *beautiful state*. It won't matter how sleep deprived you may be or what obstacles you have ahead - you'll jump out of bed with an eye looking forward to the beautiful day to come.

Figure out how to make your mornings exciting by choosing what you're excited about the next day. While you're writing down your wake up time the night before, spend 30 seconds to figure out what you can do to make sure you have the PERFECT start to the day. Maybe it's reading a few pages, meditating, or telling yourself you're going to make today one of the best days of your life.

"If you think there aren't enough hours in the day to achieve your dreams, wake up earlier in the morning." - Anonymous

Night 14

DATE _____

TONIGHT I'LL SLEEP AT: _____ & TOMORROW I'LL WAKE UP AT: _____

🪄 MAGICAL MOMENT(S) I EXPERIENCED TODAY:

_____
_____

✓ BENEFITS I FELT TODAY (CIRCLE):

| Feel Happier | More Organized | Fuller Days | Increased Productivity | More Energized | Reduced Stress |

☀ MY MORNING RITUAL TOMORROW WILL BE: *Completed?*

1. _____ ☐
2. _____ ☐
3. _____ ☐
4. _____ ☐
5. _____ ☐

Day 15

LAST NIGHT I SLEPT AT: _____ & WOKE UP TODAY AT: _____

🐎 MY MOST IMPORTANT TASK FOR TODAY IS:

_____
_____

⏱ ONE WAY I CAN IMPROVE LIFE BY 1% IS:

_____

Day 16: **Affirmations**

1. Find a quiet area where you can do this in private so you can be at ease. If you can't find a private space, say these in your head while pretending you're screaming them from a mountaintop.

2. Think of a time when you felt absolutely powerful - **when you felt on top of the world.** Tap into every emotion you had at that moment and get yourself into that state right now. How were you feeling then - Powerful? Unstoppable? Strong? Incredible!? Get into it now!!!!

3. Now feel your intensity grow tenfold! Say this with deep passion:

I see how successful people around the world understand that to get what you want in life you have to utilize every damn day to its full potential.
I will LEAP out of bed as soon as my alarm goes off at ____ A.M. and begin the day with a surge of energy.
I will use the extra morning time to do some of the best habits known to man.
My productivity, efficiency, and energy will soar through the roof by waking up with purpose and intention.

Repeat this **one more time.**

"The difference between rising at five and seven o'clock in the morning, for forty years, supposing a man to go to bed at the same hour at night, is nearly equivalent to the addition of ten years to a man's life."
- Philip Doddridge

DATE _____

Night 15

TONIGHT I'LL SLEEP AT: _____ & TOMORROW I'LL WAKE UP AT: _____

🪄 MAGICAL MOMENT(S) I EXPERIENCED TODAY:

_____

_____

✓ BENEFITS I FELT TODAY (CIRCLE):

| Feel Happier | More Organized | Fuller Days | Increased Productivity | More Energized | Reduced Stress |

☀ MY MORNING RITUAL TOMORROW WILL BE: *Completed?*

1. _____ ☐
2. _____ ☐
3. _____ ☐
4. _____ ☐
5. _____ ☐

Day 16

LAST NIGHT I SLEPT AT: _____ & WOKE UP TODAY AT: _____

🐸 MY MOST IMPORTANT TASK FOR TODAY IS:

_____

⬆ ONE WAY I CAN IMPROVE LIFE BY 1% IS:

_____

Day 17: **Pro-Tip**

Become a ninja napper.

Certain days you will feel tired and drained. It's inevitable. Taking 20 minute naps is the most efficient and effective way to boost yourself up with energy. But many of us struggle with naps - specifically with actually falling asleep.

Game-changer: **You don't need to fall asleep to benefit from a nap.**

Letting your mind drift off and relax will restore your body with energy. This 20 minute number has been backed by studies, stating it's the most efficient "bang for your buck" (for time spent napping to energy gained). Knowing this, you can use it as incentive when you set up a very early wake-up time. As sleep deprived as you may be getting up then, know you can fill yourself up with energy with quick naps during the day. Use this to push the limits of when you wake up.

How to nap properly:
1. Put your phone in airplane mode.
2. Set a timer for 20 minutes on your phone.
3. Rest your eyes for 20 minutes.
4. Once the 20 minute timer goes off, start moving quickly. Spark yourself with energy so your drowsiness dissipates. If not, you'll transition into the slower sleep cycle, taking 90+ minutes.

"A day without a nap is like a cupcake without frosting."
- Terri Guillemots

DATE _____

Night 16

TONIGHT I'LL SLEEP AT: _____ & TOMORROW I'LL WAKE UP AT: _____

🪄 MAGICAL MOMENT(S) I EXPERIENCED TODAY:

_____

_____

✓ BENEFITS I FELT TODAY (CIRCLE):

Feel Happier | More Organized | Fuller Days | Increased Productivity | More Energized | Reduced Stress

☀ MY MORNING RITUAL TOMORROW WILL BE: *Completed?*

1. _____ ☐
2. _____ ☐
3. _____ ☐
4. _____ ☐
5. _____ ☐

Day 17

LAST NIGHT I SLEPT AT: _____ & WOKE UP TODAY AT: _____

🐸 MY MOST IMPORTANT TASK FOR TODAY IS:

_____

ONE WAY I CAN IMPROVE LIFE BY 1% IS:

_____

Day 18: **Favorite Podcasts**

<u>The 5 AM Miracle with Jeff Sanders.</u>   6M+ DOWNLOADS

The 5 AM Miracle is a weekly podcast, every Monday, with one objective: to help you dominate your day before breakfast. Jeff Sanders, the host, is dedicated to helping people jump out of bed with enthusiasm, to create lifelong habits, and to tackle big goals with incredible energy.

Waking up with intention, with a plan, and with a solidified purpose can make a dramatic difference in your day, and more importantly, in your future success. Each episode either features a fascinating guest or Jeff himself jumps on the mic and dives into a new topic. The core topics include early mornings, healthy habits, personal development, and rockin' productivity!

Check out his podcast by searching "5AM Miracle" on **any podcasting app like** *iTunes*, *iHeart Radio*, *Stitcher*, or *Spreaker*.

> "Morning is an important time of day, because how you spend your morning can often tell you what kind of day you are going to have."
> - Lemony Snicket

(Have you been embracing your days of struggle? They're big blessings in disguise as you can learn so much from them).

DATE _____

Night 17

TONIGHT I'LL SLEEP AT: _____ & TOMORROW I'LL WAKE UP AT: _____

🪄 MAGICAL MOMENT(S) I EXPERIENCED TODAY:

_____

_____

✓ BENEFITS I FELT TODAY (CIRCLE):

| Feel Happier | More Organized | Fuller Days | Increased Productivity | More Energized | Reduced Stress |

☀ MY MORNING RITUAL TOMORROW WILL BE: *Completed?*

1. _____ ☐
2. _____ ☐
3. _____ ☐
4. _____ ☐
5. _____ ☐

Day 18

LAST NIGHT I SLEPT AT: _____ & WOKE UP TODAY AT: _____

🐸 MY MOST IMPORTANT TASK FOR TODAY IS:

_____

_____

⊕ ONE WAY I CAN IMPROVE LIFE BY 1% IS:

_____

Day 19: **Pro-Tip**

Use grayscale mode on your phone to break a phone addiction.

After a long day - when we're tired at night and just want to relax - it's so easy to turn to our phones for easy entertainment.

This is totally fine, though sometimes this habit can get out of line and become more destructive than it is pleasant.

One incredibly useful tip has been to put your phone into grayscale mode so that everything is black and white. This may sound simple, but by breaking the visual hook of color, your phone loses that irresistible "I just can't put this down" element. Some people even incorporate this into their nighttime routine each night before bed.

On an iPhone, you can set this as your accessibility shortcut so when you **triple tap the home button** (sorry, iPhone X users and on) it automatically switches from color to grayscale.
Set this up in: *Settings > General > Accessibility > Color Filters.*

Due to the variety of Android phones / software adoption, using Google is your best bet for finding the specific steps to do this.

"Every day may not be good, but there's something good in every day"
-Alice Morse Earle

DATE _____

Night 18

TONIGHT I'LL SLEEP AT: _____ & TOMORROW I'LL WAKE UP AT: _____

🪄 MAGICAL MOMENT(S) I EXPERIENCED TODAY:

_____
_____

✓ BENEFITS I FELT TODAY (CIRCLE):

Feel Happier — More Organized — Fuller Days — Increased Productivity — More Energized — Reduced Stress

☀ MY MORNING RITUAL TOMORROW WILL BE: *Completed?*

1. _____ ☐
2. _____ ☐
3. _____ ☐
4. _____ ☐
5. _____ ☐

Day 19

LAST NIGHT I SLEPT AT: _____ & WOKE UP TODAY AT: _____

🐎 MY MOST IMPORTANT TASK FOR TODAY IS:

_____

🧭 ONE WAY I CAN IMPROVE LIFE BY 1% IS:

_____

Day 20: **Affirmations**

1. Find a quiet area where you can do this in private so you can be at ease. If you can't find a private space, say these in your head while pretending you're screaming them from a mountaintop.

2. Think of a time when you felt absolutely powerful - **when you felt on top of the world**. Tap into every emotion you had at that moment and get yourself into that state right now. How were you feeling then - Powerful? Unstoppable? Strong? Incredible!? Get into it now!!!!

3. Now feel your intensity grow tenfold! Say this with deep passion:

By taking good care of my body with the extra time I have in the morning, I feel accomplished, vibrant, energetic and healthy throughout the day.

I am no longer negatively affected by the needs of my body because I wake up on time and make sure I feel empowered so that I can accomplish everything I set out to do.

Repeat this **one more time.**

"Dreaming or doing is a choice that will mean the difference between failure and success."
-Anonymous

Night 19

(How can we improve this journal? Email me at mikey@habitnest.com. I answer every message and love hearing feedback).

DATE _____

TONIGHT I'LL SLEEP AT: _____ & TOMORROW I'LL WAKE UP AT: _____

🪄 MAGICAL MOMENT(S) I EXPERIENCED TODAY:

_____

_____

✓ BENEFITS I FELT TODAY (CIRCLE):

- Feel Happier
- More Organized
- Fuller Days
- Increased Productivity
- More Energized
- Reduced Stress

☀ MY MORNING RITUAL TOMORROW WILL BE: *Completed?*

1. _____ ☐
2. _____ ☐
3. _____ ☐
4. _____ ☐
5. _____ ☐

Day 20

LAST NIGHT I SLEPT AT: _____ & WOKE UP TODAY AT: _____

🐎 MY MOST IMPORTANT TASK FOR TODAY IS:

_____

↑ ONE WAY I CAN IMPROVE LIFE BY 1% IS:

_____

Day 21: **Success Story**

Benjamin Franklin, of course, is one of the founding fathers of the United States. What you probably don't know is that he's also the founding father of the "to-do list".

He had some specific rules for how he started each morning. His three-hour block of morning routine stretched from 5:00 A.M. to 8:00 A.M. and included addressing "Powerful Goodness" and setting a plan for the rest of his day.

Every morning he asked himself, "What good shall I do today?"

See if any of his routines are useful for you to adopt. You can also experiment with planning your day out in the extreme hour-by-hour detail like Franklin did below:

SCHEME.		
	Hours.	
MORNING. The *Question.* What good shall I do this day?	5 6 7	Rise, wash, and address *Powerful Goodness!* Contrive day's business, and take the resolution of the day; prosecute the present study, and breakfast.
	8 9 10 11	Work.
NOON.	12 1	Read, or look over my accounts, and dine.
AFTERNOON.	2 3 4 5	Work.
EVENING. The *Question.* What good have I done to-day?	6 7 8 9	Put things in their places. Supper. Music or diversion, or conversation. Examination of the day.
NIGHT.	10 11 12 1 2 3 4	Sleep.

"Genius is 1% talent and 99% hard work." - Albert Einstein

Night 20

DATE: _____

TONIGHT I'LL SLEEP AT: _____ & TOMORROW I'LL WAKE UP AT: _____

✨ MAGICAL MOMENT(S) I EXPERIENCED TODAY:

_____

_____

✓ BENEFITS I FELT TODAY (CIRCLE):

- Feel Happier
- More Organized
- Fuller Days
- Increased Productivity
- More Energized
- Reduced Stress

☀ MY MORNING RITUAL TOMORROW WILL BE: *Completed?*

1. _____ ☐
2. _____ ☐
3. _____ ☐
4. _____ ☐
5. _____ ☐

Day 21

LAST NIGHT I SLEPT AT: _____ & WOKE UP TODAY AT: _____

🐎 MY MOST IMPORTANT TASK FOR TODAY IS:

_____

🧭 ONE WAY I CAN IMPROVE LIFE BY 1% IS:

_____

~~PHASE 2:~~ DESTROYED.

Phase 2 Recap: Days 8-21

1. What have you realized to be the most important elements for you to have a productive morning and day?

_____
_____

2. What nighttime habits should you be doing consistently?

_____
_____

3. What are some new rituals you want to experiment with?

_____
_____

4. How has being laser-focused about your mornings impacted your life?

_____
_____
_____

5. How would you feel if you stopped doing this?

_____
_____
_____

PHASE 3
DAYS 22-66

  **Phase 3**

~~Days 01-07~~ ~~Days 08-21~~ **Days 22-66+**
~~Hell Week.~~ ~~Staying Consistent.~~ **Rewiring Your Brain.**

Phase 3: Hardwiring - Retaining Interest In Your Personal Improvement

Congratulations, you've made it to Phase 3. You've shown serious commitment to the incredible future you envision for yourself.

This is a great phase to explore how to make the most out of this habit for you, personally. Most people use this phase to experiment with different routines, wakeup times, hours of sleep, etc. to tweak what works for them.

It's easy to take the benefits you're feeling for granted — it's extremely easy to fall off the wagon, especially in this phase.

Keep going strong until being a productive early riser is engrained in your DNA.

This means pushing through to stick with your commitments on your best days, your worst days, and especially the days where you just don't feel like it (those are the *most important*).

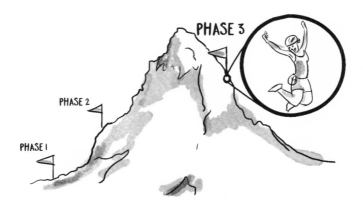

Commit.

I am INCREDIBLE.

*I've come a long way,
but the road doesn't end here.*

It's time to ingrain this habit in me forever.

*I will see this
huge challenge all the way through.*

*Mastering this habit is only the
beginning of my perpetual growth.*

_____

Nothing will stop me now.

_____   _____
Signature   Date

Phase 2 Medal Earned!

Day 22: **Pro-Tip**

<u>*Get to know your body clock.*</u>

It's weird to think that most of us don't know how much sleep our body naturally needs because we either sleep too late or sleep too much.

1. Stick to sleeping at a normal hour for a week straight (somewhere from 9:00 P.M. to 11 P.M.)

2. Allow your body to wakeup without disturbance – no snoozing, no going back to sleep after you wake up. This will give you a better sense of how much sleep your body wants as opposed to how much sleep your mind wants (oftentimes we "think" we need more sleep than we actually do).

3. Based on how much sleep you find your body needs, you can properly make decisions about when to sleep, which should be based on exactly when you want to get up in the morning.

"And when you find out what your WHY is - and your WHY gotta be deeper than you - When you find your WHY. You don't hit snooze no more! When you find your WHY. You find a way to make it happen!"
- Eric Thomas

Night 21

(Although this replaced the "Magical Moments" section, you can still use it for that if you'd like).

TONIGHT I'LL SLEEP AT: _____ & TOMORROW I'LL WAKE UP AT: _____

✏ OPENING UP ABOUT MY DAY:

_____
_____
_____
_____
_____
_____

☀ MY MORNING RITUAL TOMORROW WILL BE: *Completed?*

1. _____ ☐
2. _____ ☐
3. _____ ☐
4. _____ ☐
5. _____ ☐

Day 22

LAST NIGHT I SLEPT AT: _____ & WOKE UP TODAY AT: _____

🐸 MY MOST IMPORTANT TASK FOR TODAY IS:

_____

⊕ ONE WAY I CAN IMPROVE LIFE BY 1% IS:

_____

Day 23: **Daily Challenge**

Challenge: Take action on something that you know will make you want to cringe because it falls outside the walls of your comfort zone.

Begin to notice the comfort zone you've created for yourself. You'll realize that the little world you're living in LIMITS you in every possible way. To grow, you must break through these artificial limits.

We all have a comfort zone. Our comfort zone is who we are - things we're willing to deal with, activities we're willing engage in, people we're willing to create relationships with, etc.

The difference between you and anyone else is self-created limitations - some have bigger, more generous comfort zones, and some live in a very small world. Regardless of the size of your comfort zone, it's your biggest enemy. Comfort zones prevent us from taking action!

Nobody ever grows in a comfort zone. Ever.

We love our comfort zones because **we're afraid of failure, afraid of rejection, but most of all, afraid to disappoint ourselves** - by our own definition of what disappointment is. Your definition of disappointment is completely BS and quite frankly nobody cares if you succeed or fail. **Don't be afraid of looking vulnerable.** Take massive action and show yourself what's truly possible.

Night 22

(This new section is designed to be your open canvas for any writing, reflecting, or creative thinking!)

TONIGHT I'LL SLEEP AT: _____ & TOMORROW I'LL WAKE UP AT: _____

✏ OPENING UP ABOUT MY DAY:

_____
_____
_____
_____
_____
_____

☀ MY MORNING RITUAL TOMORROW WILL BE: *Completed?*

1. _____ ☐
2. _____ ☐
3. _____ ☐
4. _____ ☐
5. _____ ☐

Day 23

LAST NIGHT I SLEPT AT: _____ & WOKE UP TODAY AT: _____

🐸 MY MOST IMPORTANT TASK FOR TODAY IS:

_____

⏱ ONE WAY I CAN IMPROVE LIFE BY 1% IS:

_____

Day 24: **Affirmations**

1. Find a quiet area where you can do this in private so you can be at ease. If you can't find a private space, say these in your head while pretending you're screaming them from a mountaintop.

2. Think of a time when you felt absolutely powerful - **when you felt on top of the world**. Tap into every emotion you had at that moment and get yourself into that state right now. How were you feeling then - Powerful? Unstoppable? Strong? Incredible!? Get into it now!!!!

3. Now feel your intensity grow tenfold! Say this with deep passion:

I am fulfilling my life's mission to master my mornings and boosting the quality of my entire day. I will stop at nothing to make this a reality for myself. My life will reach a whole new level it's never seen before!

I am fulfilling my mission of having the most productive days of my life. The extra time I receive from being a laser-focused early riser gives me a secret edge to conquer my day.

Repeat this **one more time.**

EVERY PASSING DAY IT BECOMES EASIER AND EASIER TO WAKE UP EARLY

"Affirmations are like seed planted in soil. Poor soil, poor growth. Rich soil, abundant growth. The more you choose to think thoughts that make you feel good, the quicker the affirmations work." - Louise L. Hay

Night 23

(Some people use this to think of ways to improve this habit in the long-run. Others to reflect on their days).

TONIGHT I'LL SLEEP AT: _____ & TOMORROW I'LL WAKE UP AT: _____

OPENING UP ABOUT MY DAY:

_____
_____
_____
_____
_____
_____

MY MORNING RITUAL TOMORROW WILL BE: *Completed?*

1. _____ ☐
2. _____ ☐
3. _____ ☐
4. _____ ☐
5. _____ ☐

Day 24

LAST NIGHT I SLEPT AT: _____ & WOKE UP TODAY AT: _____

MY MOST IMPORTANT TASK FOR TODAY IS:

_____

ONE WAY I CAN IMPROVE LIFE BY 1% IS:

_____

Day 25: **Super Read**

Amazon Reviews: 192

★★★★★ 4.3

Title: Wake Up Successful - How to Increase Your Energy and Achieve Any Goal with a Morning Routine
Author: S.J. Scott

First of all, S.J. Scott is one of the most active authors in the personal development space with tons of incredible content. This is one of his many books, jam-packed with strategies, tips, routines, examples, and suggested rituals. In fact, we used his *Master Evernote* book to organize a lot of our notes in compiling this journal.

In *Wake Up Successful* you'll learn how to live every day like it's your last. No longer will you stumble out of bed and waste the first few hours. Instead, you'll learn how to start the day by creating energy and using this power to focus on ONE breakthrough goal that will make a difference in your life.

A morning routine is simple and effective. It's easy to tailor to your unique goals. And, best of all, it's tested. Inside this book, you'll discover the proven strategies to help you get the most out of those precious first few hours.

"Simply wake up every morning a better person than when [you] went to bed." - Sidney Poitier

Night 24

TONIGHT I'LL SLEEP AT: _____ & TOMORROW I'LL WAKE UP AT: _____

✎ OPENING UP ABOUT MY DAY:

(Idea: use this as a place to write out a nighttime routine for yourself).

_____
_____
_____
_____
_____
_____

☀ MY MORNING RITUAL TOMORROW WILL BE: *Completed?*

1. _____ ☐
2. _____ ☐
3. _____ ☐
4. _____ ☐
5. _____ ☐

Day 25

LAST NIGHT I SLEPT AT: _____ & WOKE UP TODAY AT: _____

🐸 MY MOST IMPORTANT TASK FOR TODAY IS:

_____

⊙ ONE WAY I CAN IMPROVE LIFE BY 1% IS:

_____

Day 26: **Daily Challenge**

Maintain consistency throughout the weekend.

On the weekend, we have a completely different schedule than during the rest of the week. We sleep late, we do completely different tasks. The problem is - your body doesn't know that. To your body, Monday morning and Sunday morning are the same exact thing.

If you're waking up at 5 A.M. throughout the week and then begin sleeping very late on the weekends, you'll confuse your body and your system. From this inconsistency, it's going to be much harder for you to start waking up early in upcoming weekdays.

If waking up early on weekends means you become a bit sleep deprived, it is oftentimes worth it. You can make up for it with napping in the day. Plus the benefit of remaining consistent will carry on throughout the upcoming days, weeks, and months ahead.

For the sake of consistency, treat weekends and weekdays the same. Attempt making weekdays and weekends follow the same routine – at least for 1 week straight.

"For the past 33 years, I have looked in the mirror every morning and asked myself: 'If today were the last day of my life, would I want to do what I am about to do today?' And whenever the answer has been no for too many days in a row, I know I need to change something." - Steve Jobs

Night 25

TONIGHT I'LL SLEEP AT: _____ & TOMORROW I'LL WAKE UP AT: _____

✏️ OPENING UP ABOUT MY DAY:

_____
_____
_____
_____
_____

(Feel free to experiment with new rituals as you advance through this habit).

☀️ MY MORNING RITUAL TOMORROW WILL BE: *Completed?*

1. _____ ☐
2. _____ ☐
3. _____ ☐
4. _____ ☐
5. _____ ☐

Day 26

LAST NIGHT I SLEPT AT: _____ & WOKE UP TODAY AT: _____

🐎 MY MOST IMPORTANT TASK FOR TODAY IS:

_____

⊕ ONE WAY I CAN IMPROVE LIFE BY 1% IS:

_____

Day 27: **Favorite Podcasts**

Smart Passive Income Podcast with Pat Flynn. 33M+ DOWNLOADS

The Smart Passive Income Podcast is a top-ranking business podcast on iTunes and was featured in the New York Times! The host, Pat Flynn, has an incredible blog called *The Smart Passive Income Blog.* In 2008 he had a 9-5 job that eventually led him to being laid off. He decided to work for himself from home and has been able to earn more money and work less (with more flexible) hours — which in the end allows him to be home and spend time with family. Oh yeah, and he discloses his income reports every month on his blog — pretty amazing, right?

In episode #140 called, "Productivity and the Early Morning Routine with Hal Elrod," you'll be able to get some incredibly valuable information for your morning routine and how it can help your productivity.

To check out his podcast, search for: *Smart Passive Income* on **any podcasting app like** *iTunes*, *iHeart Radio*, *Stitcher*, or *Spreaker*.

- Over 18 million downloads!
- 75,000 people on his newsletter!
- Top-ranking business podcast in iTunes

"Eating right and taking the time to slow down and plan in the morning is crucial to a productive day."
– David Moore

Night 26

TONIGHT I'LL SLEEP AT: _____ & TOMORROW I'LL WAKE UP AT: _____

✎ OPENING UP ABOUT MY DAY:

_____
_____
_____
_____

(To test new habits you're interested in, you could give yourself a mini "3-day challenge" to see if you like them).

☀ MY MORNING RITUAL TOMORROW WILL BE: *Completed?*

1. _____ ☐
2. _____ ☐
3. _____ ☐
4. _____ ☐
5. _____ ☐

Day 27

LAST NIGHT I SLEPT AT: _____ & WOKE UP TODAY AT: _____

🐸 MY MOST IMPORTANT TASK FOR TODAY IS:

_____

◉ ONE WAY I CAN IMPROVE LIFE BY 1% IS:

_____

Day 28: **Affirmations**

1. Find a quiet area where you can do this in private so you can be at ease. If you can't find a private space, say these in your head while pretending you're screaming them from a mountaintop.

2. Think of a time when you felt absolutely powerful - **when you felt on top of the world**. Tap into every emotion you had at that moment and get yourself into that state right now. How were you feeling then - Powerful? Unstoppable? Strong? Incredible!? Get into it now!!!!

3. Now feel your intensity grow tenfold! Say this with deep passion:

Every day I do my morning routine, I attract beauty, sparks of fun, and surges of happiness to my life. The more I own my mornings, the more pure goodness will flow into my life effortlessly.

By mastering myself and my life, I skyrocket the quality of my life. My passion deeply outweighs any of the challenges I will face on this journey. I own this. I can do this, I can do this easily, and I can do this now.

Repeat this **one more time**.

I WAKE UP EARLY AND MAKE SURE I FEEL PERFECT SO THAT I CAN ACCOMPLISH EVERYTHING I SET OUT TO DO

Night 27

TONIGHT I'LL SLEEP AT: _____ & TOMORROW I'LL WAKE UP AT: _____

✏️ OPENING UP ABOUT MY DAY:

_____
_____
_____
_____
_____
_____
_____

☀️ MY MORNING RITUAL TOMORROW WILL BE: *Completed?*

1. _____ ☐
2. _____ ☐
3. _____ ☐
4. _____ ☐
5. _____ ☐

Day 28

LAST NIGHT I SLEPT AT: _____ & WOKE UP TODAY AT: _____

🐸 MY MOST IMPORTANT TASK FOR TODAY IS:

_____

🧭 ONE WAY I CAN IMPROVE LIFE BY 1% IS:

_____

Day 29: **Favorite Resources**

Product: Sleep Cycle™ (iPhone or android App)
Cost: $0.99.
Note: we have no affiliation with Sleep Cycle™. We just love the app.

Feeling fresh the moment you open your eyes is all about timing. The Sleep Cycle™ alarm clock tracks your sleep patterns and wakes you up when you're in a light sleep state. Waking up during light sleep feels like waking up naturally rested without an alarm clock — it's a pretty amazing feeling, and the app works surprisingly accurately too.

1. You go through phases when you sleep (first light sleep, then deep sleep, then Rapid Eye Movement sleep) and your movements in sleep vary with each phase.
2. The app tracks your movements (or sounds) to wake you up during the light phase of your sleep using a 30 minute alarm window of your choice.
3. Your sleep patterns are tracked on a graph to show you at what points in the night you are in either light, deep or REM sleep.

Download: www.sleepcycle.com

"I get up every morning and it's going to be a great day. You never know when it's going to be over so I refuse to have a bad day."
- Paul Henderson

Night 28

TONIGHT I'LL SLEEP AT: _____ & TOMORROW I'LL WAKE UP AT: _____

✎ OPENING UP ABOUT MY DAY:

_____
_____
_____
_____
_____
_____

☀ MY MORNING RITUAL TOMORROW WILL BE: *Completed?*

1. _____ ☐
2. _____ ☐
3. _____ ☐
4. _____ ☐
5. _____ ☐

Day 29

LAST NIGHT I SLEPT AT: _____ & WOKE UP TODAY AT: _____

🐎 MY MOST IMPORTANT TASK FOR TODAY IS:

_____

⊕ ONE WAY I CAN IMPROVE LIFE BY 1% IS:

_____

Day 30: **Success Story**

<u>Gerry Laybourne, Oxygen™ Channel Co-Founder; Oxygen™ Sold: $925M</u>

The founder of Oxygen™ is awake by 6 A.M. and out of the house within half an hour. If you get up early enough, she may even give you some life or business advice! The serial entrepreneur told Yahoo! Finance:

"Once or twice a week, I go for a walk in Central Park with a young person seeking my advice. This is my way of helping bring along the next generation. And if someone is up early in the morning then they are serious about life. I can't take time at the office to do this, but doing it in the morning allows me to get exercise and stay connected with young people at the same time."

Similar to Laybourne's routine, what's an activity you can do in your mornings that will either get you more exercise or give back to the world in some way?

"Few ever lived to old age, and fewer still ever became distinguished, who were not in the habit of early rising." - John Todd

Night 29

TONIGHT I'LL SLEEP AT: _____ & TOMORROW I'LL WAKE UP AT: _____

OPENING UP ABOUT MY DAY:

_____
_____
_____
_____
_____
_____
_____

MY MORNING RITUAL TOMORROW WILL BE:

Completed?

1. _____ ☐
2. _____ ☐
3. _____ ☐
4. _____ ☐
5. _____ ☐

Day 30

LAST NIGHT I SLEPT AT: _____ & WOKE UP TODAY AT: _____

MY MOST IMPORTANT TASK FOR TODAY IS:

_____

ONE WAY I CAN IMPROVE LIFE BY 1% IS:

_____

Day 31: **Affirmations**

1. Find a quiet area where you can do this in private so you can be at ease. If you can't find a private space, say these in your head while pretending you're screaming them from a mountaintop.

2. Think of a time when you felt absolutely powerful - **when you felt on top of the world.** Tap into every emotion you had at that moment and get yourself into that state right now. How were you feeling then - Powerful? Unstoppable? Strong? Incredible!? Get into it now!!!!

3. Now feel your intensity grow tenfold! Say this with deep passion:

I will wake up on time every day no matter how hard it is. I will wake up full of energy and purpose as soon as I hear the sound of my alarm.

Because I wake up early and jump into my morning routine, I serve as a shining example who inspires others to conquer their mornings.

Repeat this **one more time**.

"I used to love night best but the older I get the more treasures and hope and joy I find in mornings." - Terri Guillemots

Night 30

TONIGHT I'LL SLEEP AT: _____ & TOMORROW I'LL WAKE UP AT: _____

✏️ OPENING UP ABOUT MY DAY:

_____
_____
_____
_____
_____
_____
_____

☀️ MY MORNING RITUAL TOMORROW WILL BE: *Completed?*

1. _____ ☐
2. _____ ☐
3. _____ ☐
4. _____ ☐
5. _____ ☐

Day 31

LAST NIGHT I SLEPT AT: _____ & WOKE UP TODAY AT: _____

🐸 MY MOST IMPORTANT TASK FOR TODAY IS:

_____

⏱ ONE WAY I CAN IMPROVE LIFE BY 1% IS:

_____

Day 32: **Pro-Tip**

<u>*Write down your desired wake up time.*</u>

Reading that above statement, you may wonder how this will help you wake up early. The simple fact is, that writing down the time you want to wake up makes your goal tangible and REAL for you. It creates a physical expectation of yourself that's now written out into the world (instead of just staying in your mind). This makes it harder for you to break it.

When you write down what time you want to wake up the night before, you better internalize the information/goal. Your mindset switches a little bit. The night before, just write down on a piece of paper, "I want to wake up at..." and fill in the blank - whether it's 5, 8, or 11 A.M. **Write it down.** It's going to be better ingrained in your brain; your mindset is going to be different.

When it's dark outside, you're waking up, and all the voices in your head are saying, "Don't wake up, go back to bed," you need to use every piece of ammunition you have.

"I usually get up at 5 or 5:15am...I am not a big sleeper and never have been. Life is too exciting to sleep." - Howard Schultz

Night 31

TONIGHT I'LL SLEEP AT: _____ & TOMORROW I'LL WAKE UP AT: _____

✏️ OPENING UP ABOUT MY DAY:

_____
_____
_____
_____
_____
_____
_____

☀️ MY MORNING RITUAL TOMORROW WILL BE: *Completed?*

1. _____ ☐
2. _____ ☐
3. _____ ☐
4. _____ ☐
5. _____ ☐

Day 32

LAST NIGHT I SLEPT AT: _____ & WOKE UP TODAY AT: _____

🐸 MY MOST IMPORTANT TASK FOR TODAY IS:

_____

🎯 ONE WAY I CAN IMPROVE LIFE BY 1% IS:

_____

Day 33: **Daily Challenge**

Build the habit of shifting between "off" and "on" days

As we covered before, it's very common to have failed and missed days as you grow a morning routine in your life. One critical value point we hope you take away from this experience is building the habit of **moving FROM a point of failure** (missing a day or multiple days) **BACK to the effort of rebuilding this habit.**

That is where the magic happens.

Arguably, missing days make up a critical component of being realistic that you likely won't wake up at 5am every day for the rest of your life, yet that whenever you want to, you can call back on your ability to SHIFT BACK into that habit.

That is what this journal will provide you - the ability to choose and call upon this habit whenever and however often you'd like.

Action step: The next time you fail, remind yourself the immense long-term value of getting back on track and rebuilding that sill.

"Let today be the day you give up who you've been for who you can become." - Hal Elrod

Night 32

TONIGHT I'LL SLEEP AT: _____ & TOMORROW I'LL WAKE UP AT: _____

✏️ OPENING UP ABOUT MY DAY:

_____
_____
_____
_____
_____
_____
_____

☀️ MY MORNING RITUAL TOMORROW WILL BE: *Completed?*

1. _____ ☐
2. _____ ☐
3. _____ ☐
4. _____ ☐
5. _____ ☐

Day 33

LAST NIGHT I SLEPT AT: _____ & WOKE UP TODAY AT: _____

🐸 MY MOST IMPORTANT TASK FOR TODAY IS:

_____

🎯 ONE WAY I CAN IMPROVE LIFE BY 1% IS:

_____

Day 34: **Success Story**

Bob Iger, Disney™ CEO; Total Compensation in 2014: $46.5 M

Iger gets up at 4:30 every morning. He takes the quiet time to do a number of things together, such as reading the papers, exercising, listening to music, looking at email, and watching TV all at the same time. This CEO is multitasking before the sun comes out.

He said in order to keep the company pushing out some of the greatest films he has to wake up at 4:30 A.M. From there he's off to the gym at 5, and at the office by 6. For Iger, it's really about recharging his batteries and clearing his mind.

"I get up at 4:30 in the morning, seven days a week, no matter where I am in the world." - Bob Iger

Iger does a lot with his mornings - but the most impressive piece is just how consistent he is, waking up at 4:30 A.M. even when traveling. Qualities like this are why he's able to successfully run such a huge yet magical corporation.

"Think in the morning. Act in the noon. Eat in the evening. Sleep in the night." - *William Blake*

Night 33

TONIGHT I'LL SLEEP AT: _____ & TOMORROW I'LL WAKE UP AT: _____

✎ OPENING UP ABOUT MY DAY:

_____
_____
_____
_____
_____
_____
_____

(3-day challenge idea: meditate for 3 minutes a day).

☀ MY MORNING RITUAL TOMORROW WILL BE: *Completed?*

1. _____ ☐
2. _____ ☐
3. _____ ☐
4. _____ ☐
5. _____ ☐

Day 34

LAST NIGHT I SLEPT AT: _____ & WOKE UP TODAY AT: _____

🐸 MY MOST IMPORTANT TASK FOR TODAY IS:

_____

⊕ ONE WAY I CAN IMPROVE LIFE BY 1% IS:

_____

Day 35: **Affirmations**

1. Find a quiet area where you can do this in private so you can be at ease. If you can't find a private space, say these in your head while pretending you're screaming them from a mountaintop.

2. Think of a time when you felt absolutely powerful - **when you felt on top of the world**. Tap into every emotion you had at that moment and get yourself into that state right now. How were you feeling then - Powerful? Unstoppable? Strong? Incredible!? Get into it now!!!!

3. Now feel your intensity grow tenfold! Say this with deep passion:

By waking up on time I can knock out my biggest, most important, life-changing tasks of the day early on. By knocking out big tasks early on, I create positive momentum that fuels me for the day.

All this fills me up with mental clarity and peace of mind every day, which in turn helps me master every area of my life.

Repeat this **one more time.**

"Life is waking up an hour early to live an hour more."
- Anonymous

Night 34

TONIGHT I'LL SLEEP AT: _____ & TOMORROW I'LL WAKE UP AT: _____

✏️ OPENING UP ABOUT MY DAY:

_____
_____
_____
_____
_____
_____

☀️ MY MORNING RITUAL TOMORROW WILL BE: *Completed?*

1. _____ ☐
2. _____ ☐
3. _____ ☐
4. _____ ☐
5. _____ ☐

Day 35

LAST NIGHT I SLEPT AT: _____ & WOKE UP TODAY AT: _____

🐸 MY MOST IMPORTANT TASK FOR TODAY IS:

_____

🎯 ONE WAY I CAN IMPROVE LIFE BY 1% IS:

_____

Day 36: **Success Story**

John Paul DeJoria, Co-founder of Patron™; Net Worth: $2.8 B

DeJoria begins every single morning, no matter where and when, with about five minutes of quiet reflection to "just be." He spends the time being grateful for what he has.

Immediately after he gathers himself, DeJoria begins his day by checking his calendar for the day and knocking out important phone calls and meetings. The co-founder of Patron™ surprisingly "doesn't do email." He was quoted saying, "I know, I've been told I'm a bit old school, but it all gets done just the way I need it to. It allows me to focus on the important things that need my attention."

Can you incorporate gratitude or writing into your morning routine? Or perhaps spend some time to organize what tasks you will tackle each day and in what order.

"The time just before dawn contains the most energy of all hours of the day. This has helped me become an early riser and an early doer...When I wake to see that it's light out already, I feel the world has started without me." - Terri Guillemets

Night 35

TONIGHT I'LL SLEEP AT: _____ & TOMORROW I'LL WAKE UP AT: _____

✏️ OPENING UP ABOUT MY DAY:

_____
_____
_____
_____
_____
_____

☀️ MY MORNING RITUAL TOMORROW WILL BE: *Completed?*

1. _____ ☐
2. _____ ☐
3. _____ ☐
4. _____ ☐
5. _____ ☐

Day 36

LAST NIGHT I SLEPT AT: _____ & WOKE UP TODAY AT: _____

🐸 MY MOST IMPORTANT TASK FOR TODAY IS:

_____

🧭 ONE WAY I CAN IMPROVE LIFE BY 1% IS:

_____

Day 37: **Daily Challenge**

Challenge: Think about what the image of perfection you've created for yourself is... Now realize that you may NEVER fit that image! Instead, be yourself and love yourself for all that you are.

Most of us subconsciously judge ourselves for not fitting this image of perfection whenever we slip up or struggle even the slightest bit. This is a horrendous activity that will lead you to unhappiness, a spiral of guilt, a feeling of unworthiness, and freeze you in inactivity.

What does this cycle do to help you succeed and live a happy life? **NOTHING.** The truth is the quicker you can do the following, the happier your life will be day after day.

Anytime you feel you're not in a state of pure happiness:

1. Determine what mistakes you made and what went wrong.
2. Identify what you can learn from this and apply it to your future.
3. **Forgive yourself.** Now forgive yourself again.
4. Love yourself for exactly what you are right now.
5. Now **move forward full speed ahead** with what you've learned.

It doesn't matter if it takes you 50 learning cycles or 5 years of mistakes — the second you lose is when you throw on that useless guilt and unnecessary negative emotions because you're trashing your quality of life... and increasing your quality of life is the whole point you're doing this all in the first place!

Night 36

TONIGHT I'LL SLEEP AT: _____ & TOMORROW I'LL WAKE UP AT: _____

OPENING UP ABOUT MY DAY:

_____
_____
_____
_____
_____
_____
_____

MY MORNING RITUAL TOMORROW WILL BE: *Completed?*

1. _____ ☐
2. _____ ☐
3. _____ ☐
4. _____ ☐
5. _____ ☐

Day 37

LAST NIGHT I SLEPT AT: _____ & WOKE UP TODAY AT: _____

MY MOST IMPORTANT TASK FOR TODAY IS:

_____

ONE WAY I CAN IMPROVE LIFE BY 1% IS:

_____

Day 38: **Favorite Podcasts**

Reviews: 395
★★★★★ 4.5

Morning Coach Personal Development Podcast.

This podcast hosted by JB Glossinger is designed to be outstandingly motivating. It's all about helping you become the best version of you.

The main topics include health, abundance, manifestation, wealth, meditation, energy and the law of attraction. There is no better way to begin every single day than by listening to this podcast and setting yourself up for happiness, achievement, financial success and pure joy. It's all about the practice of simple and easy to use personal development and life coaching principles.

Check out his podcast by searching "Morning Coach" on **any podcasting app like** *iTunes*, *iHeart Radio*, *Stitcher*, or *Spreaker*.

"A dream doesn't become reality through magic; it takes sweat, determination and hard work. The price of success is hard work, dedication to the job at hand, and the determination that whether we win or lose, we have applied the best of ourselves to the task at hand."
- Vince Lombardi

Night 37

TONIGHT I'LL SLEEP AT: _____ & TOMORROW I'LL WAKE UP AT: _____

✏️ OPENING UP ABOUT MY DAY:

_____
_____
_____
_____
_____
_____
_____

☀️ MY MORNING RITUAL TOMORROW WILL BE: *Completed?*

1. _____ ☐
2. _____ ☐
3. _____ ☐
4. _____ ☐
5. _____ ☐

Day 38

LAST NIGHT I SLEPT AT: _____ & WOKE UP TODAY AT: _____

🐸 MY MOST IMPORTANT TASK FOR TODAY IS:

_____

⏱ ONE WAY I CAN IMPROVE LIFE BY 1% IS:

_____

Day 39: **Pro-Tip**

Put your phone/alarm away from your bed to force you to get up.

Put your alarm clock or phone (if you use it as an alarm clock) far away from you bed. In the mornings, one of the most crucial steps to getting going is simply stepping out of bed. Getting up to turn off your alarm is a no-brainer solution.

In the mornings, the second you get to your phone to turn off your alarm, do NOT allow yourself to even touch your bed again. Keep moving and go to the bathroom to brush your teeth or begin your morning routine.

Bonus Benefit: By having your phone away from your bed, it provides a layer of security against wasting time using your phone before bedtime.

"I never knew a man come to greatness or eminence who lay abed late in the morning." - Johnathan Swift

Night 38

TONIGHT I'LL SLEEP AT: _____ & TOMORROW I'LL WAKE UP AT: _____

✎ OPENING UP ABOUT MY DAY:

_____
_____
_____
_____
_____
_____
_____

☀ MY MORNING RITUAL TOMORROW WILL BE: *Completed?*

1. _____ ☐
2. _____ ☐
3. _____ ☐
4. _____ ☐
5. _____ ☐

Day 39

LAST NIGHT I SLEPT AT: _____ & WOKE UP TODAY AT: _____

🐎 MY MOST IMPORTANT TASK FOR TODAY IS:

_____

⏱ ONE WAY I CAN IMPROVE LIFE BY 1% IS:

_____

Day 40: **Daily Challenge**

<u>*Challenge: Think deeply about the direct relationship between the actions you take today and your future.*</u>

Newsflash: *You are exactly a compilation of your past actions. The future version of you is exactly a compilation of the actions you take starting today.*

How do you envision yourself in the future? Successful? What actions have you taken the last month that is in direct relation to the future version of yourself you are envisioning?

One of the problems is that we believe in the possibility of a future version of ourselves that's different from who we are in this moment. We imagine that the future version of us will magically begin to take the actions towards the goals we have today, without us altering our actions today.

Our brains function off our habits. Our habits function off our actions. Our actions can only come from from the present moment.

Understand that our dream lives only exist if we change our behaviors TODAY.

Night 39

TONIGHT I'LL SLEEP AT: _____ & TOMORROW I'LL WAKE UP AT: _____

✎ OPENING UP ABOUT MY DAY:

_____
_____
_____
_____
_____
_____
_____

☀ MY MORNING RITUAL TOMORROW WILL BE: *Completed?*

1. _____ ☐
2. _____ ☐
3. _____ ☐
4. _____ ☐
5. _____ ☐

Day 40

LAST NIGHT I SLEPT AT: _____ & WOKE UP TODAY AT: _____

🐸 MY MOST IMPORTANT TASK FOR TODAY IS:

_____

⊕ ONE WAY I CAN IMPROVE LIFE BY 1% IS:

_____

Day 41: **Pro-Tip**

Don't check your email in the mornings!

Email is notorious for being one of the most time-sucking, distracting tools out there. Here's why:
1. Email is a ***reactive*** tool used to respond to others. The majority of the time, it does not create any new opportunities for us.
2. Each email notification we receive throughout our day distracts us from whatever task we're working on (***this is a huge cost***).
3. When checking email on the go from our phones, it usually takes us much longer to go through (due to slower mobile typing speeds and a lack of navigating many webpages quickly).

The mornings are a magical time you can use for creative work. Leave mindless email until later in the day. One amazing tool you can use for this is InboxPause, which only pushes e-mails to your inbox at times you specify.

Superhero option: turn off e-mail notifications altogether and only check it twice a day using InboxPause.

"There was never a night or problem that could defeat sunrise or hope."
- Bernard Williams

Night 40

TONIGHT I'LL SLEEP AT: _____ & TOMORROW I'LL WAKE UP AT: _____

OPENING UP ABOUT MY DAY:

_____
_____
_____
_____
_____
_____
_____

MY MORNING RITUAL TOMORROW WILL BE: *Completed?*

(3-day challenge idea: stretch for 2 minutes each morning).

1. _____ ☐
2. _____ ☐
3. _____ ☐
4. _____ ☐
5. _____ ☐

Day 41

LAST NIGHT I SLEPT AT: _____ & WOKE UP TODAY AT: _____

MY MOST IMPORTANT TASK FOR TODAY IS:

_____

ONE WAY I CAN IMPROVE LIFE BY 1% IS:

_____

Day 42: **Favorite Podcasts**

The Tim Ferriss Show.

300M+ DOWNLOADS

Tim Ferriss' podcast has been rated the #1 podcast in the world multiple times. In it he deconstructs the world-class performers from eclectic areas (investing, sports, business, art, etc.) to extract the tactics, tools, and routines you can use.

He's interviewed past guests such as Arnold Schwarzenegger, Jamie Foxx, Edward Norton, Tony Robbins, Maria Popova, Peter Thiel, Marc Andreessen, Amanda Palmer, Malcolm Gladwell, & more.

Towards the end of each podcast episode, Ferriss asks podcast guests what their morning routine consists of. It serves as a great example to see what some of the world's leaders are doing each morning.

Check out his podcast on *iTunes, iHeart Radio, Stitcher*, or *Spreaker*. To find it you can simply search "Tim Ferriss".

"The older generation thought nothing of getting up at five every morning and the younger generation doesn't think much of it either."
– John J. Welsh

Night 41

TONIGHT I'LL SLEEP AT: _____ & TOMORROW I'LL WAKE UP AT: _____

✎ OPENING UP ABOUT MY DAY:

_____
_____
_____
_____
_____
_____
_____

☀ MY MORNING RITUAL TOMORROW WILL BE: *Completed?*

1. _____ ☐
2. _____ ☐
3. _____ ☐
4. _____ ☐
5. _____ ☐

Day 42

LAST NIGHT I SLEPT AT: _____ & WOKE UP TODAY AT: _____

🐸 MY MOST IMPORTANT TASK FOR TODAY IS:

_____

⊕ ONE WAY I CAN IMPROVE LIFE BY 1% IS:

_____

Day 43: **Affirmations**

1. Find a quiet area where you can do this in private so you can be at ease. If you can't find a private space, say these in your head while pretending you're screaming them from a mountaintop.

2. Think of a time when you felt absolutely powerful - **when you felt on top of the world.** Tap into every emotion you had at that moment and get yourself into that state right now. How were you feeling then - Powerful? Unstoppable? Strong? Incredible!? Get into it now!!!!

3. Now feel your intensity grow tenfold! Say this with deep passion:

My productivity, efficiency, and energy will soar through the roof by waking up with purpose and intention.
By waking up at ____A.M., I will accomplish important and necessary tasks that lead me directly to accomplishing my life goals.
I must master this element of my life because of how much value it will add to my life and to everybody I interact with. I <u>will</u> own this.

Repeat this **one more time.**

"No matter how bad things are, you can at least be happy that you woke up this morning." – D. L Hugely

Night 42

TONIGHT I'LL SLEEP AT: _____ & TOMORROW I'LL WAKE UP AT: _____

✏️ OPENING UP ABOUT MY DAY:

_____
_____
_____
_____
_____
_____
_____

☀️ MY MORNING RITUAL TOMORROW WILL BE: *Completed?*

1. _____ ☐
2. _____ ☐
3. _____ ☐
4. _____ ☐
5. _____ ☐

Day 43

LAST NIGHT I SLEPT AT: _____ & WOKE UP TODAY AT: _____

🐎 MY MOST IMPORTANT TASK FOR TODAY IS:

_____

🎯 ONE WAY I CAN IMPROVE LIFE BY 1% IS:

_____

Day 44: Pro-Tip + Affirmation

Set your intent for the morning the night before.

Imagine this: It's 11:30 P.M., you need to get up at 5 A.M. You feel the pain of only getting 5.5 hours of sleep - you've instantly communicated your dissatisfaction with your body and mind. You're now at a disadvantage —you've decided you're going to be tired and groggy due to inadequate sleep.

Try saying this out loud instead: *I will be waking up at 5:30 A.M. with an abundance of energy. I will spring out of bed ready to crush the incredible day in front of me. 5.5 hours of sleep is the perfect amount I need to be fresh and energized to have an awesome and productive day. I am grateful for the 5.5 hours of sleep I'm about to get because it is the perfect amount of sleep I need to have an amazing day!*

This "positive thinking" approach may sound like mumbo jumbo, but genuinely do it for one night. Tailor that message however you need, but keep it positive. Send good vibes to your body, mind and heart to wake up a **winner**. If you're upset the night before regarding the amount of sleep you're about to get, you've already lost.

"Keep your dreams alive. Understand to achieve anything requires faith and belief in yourself, vision, hard work, determination, and dedication. Remember all things are possible for those who believe." - Gail Devers

Night 43

TONIGHT I'LL SLEEP AT: _____ & TOMORROW I'LL WAKE UP AT: _____

✏️ OPENING UP ABOUT MY DAY:

_____
_____
_____
_____
_____
_____
_____

☀️ MY MORNING RITUAL TOMORROW WILL BE: *Completed?*

1. _____ ☐
2. _____ ☐
3. _____ ☐
4. _____ ☐
5. _____ ☐

Day 44

LAST NIGHT I SLEPT AT: _____ & WOKE UP TODAY AT: _____

🐎 MY MOST IMPORTANT TASK FOR TODAY IS:

_____

⏲️ ONE WAY I CAN IMPROVE LIFE BY 1% IS:

_____

Day 45: **Pro-Tip**

<u>*Set your lights out (aka going to bed) time early in the day.*</u>
<u>*Plan your day around getting to bed at that time.*</u>

Setting the time you will be in bed by is a very powerful tool, as simple as it is. This is great for days you have a more routine schedule (usually weeknights) as weekends can be a bit erratic.

Setting this time does a few things:

1. It helps you plan out the remainder of your day (i.e. how many hours you have left in the day to do what you want to do).
2. It guides you with what time you need to start preparing for bed to make sure you're ready on time.
3. It prevents you from following a string of distractions during nighttime.
4. It gives you a set time to read (reading and sleeping should be the only things that you allow yourself to do).
5. It almost guarantees your success for waking up early as your morning success if directly linked to what you do at night.

"Don't just drag out of bed every morning. Get alive and awaken your mind and body for the gift of a brand new day gift wrapped with sunlight and air. Not just another ordinary day, it is the day of new opportunities." – Phoebe Kites

Night 44

TONIGHT I'LL SLEEP AT: _____ & TOMORROW I'LL WAKE UP AT: _____

✎ OPENING UP ABOUT MY DAY:

_____
_____
_____
_____
_____
_____
_____

☀ MY MORNING RITUAL TOMORROW WILL BE: *Completed?*

1. _____ ☐
2. _____ ☐
3. _____ ☐
4. _____ ☐
5. _____ ☐

Day 45

LAST NIGHT I SLEPT AT: _____ & WOKE UP TODAY AT: _____

🐸 MY MOST IMPORTANT TASK FOR TODAY IS:

_____

⏱ ONE WAY I CAN IMPROVE LIFE BY 1% IS:

_____

Day 46: **Success Story**

Tim Cook, Apple™ CEO; Net Worth: $785 million.

The CEO of Apple™ is known for getting up and sending out company emails at 4:30 in the morning. By 5 A.M. he can be found in the gym. And he works late too, priding himself on being the first in the office and the last out. He's said to have extremely high energy levels — and he himself attributes much of his success to being an early riser and getting necessary tasks done before he goes to work.

On March 9, 2015 he tweeted at 5:31 A.M. (probably after his morning workout), "Got some extra rest for today's event. Slept in 'til 4:30." *What a beast.*

"Don't underestimate the power of thoughts and words. What you tell yourself every morning will set your mind and life on success."
- Nina Bolivares

Night 45

TONIGHT I'LL SLEEP AT: _____ & TOMORROW I'LL WAKE UP AT: _____

✎ OPENING UP ABOUT MY DAY:

_____
_____
_____
_____
_____
_____

☀ MY MORNING RITUAL TOMORROW WILL BE: *Completed?*

1. _____ ☐
2. _____ ☐
3. _____ ☐
4. _____ ☐
5. _____ ☐

Day 46

LAST NIGHT I SLEPT AT: _____ & WOKE UP TODAY AT: _____

🐸 MY MOST IMPORTANT TASK FOR TODAY IS:

_____

⊙ ONE WAY I CAN IMPROVE LIFE BY 1% IS:

_____

Day 47: **Daily Challenge**

<u>*Challenge: Learn to discriminate against habitual thoughts that limit your quality and potential in life.*</u>

We ordinarily take ourselves to be our thoughts — the flow of that thought is **always** active, constantly creating the context and substance of what we're experiencing in our lives.

We are habitual animals; we are **association machines**. As we move through life, we access every association that has been created in our past related to what we're currently faced with.

The problem: when our associations are triggered through our thoughts, there isn't an active thinking process. <u>Our past</u> (the network of associations built based on previous experiences) answers life for us.

To create positive change, we must detach from automatic thoughts that **happen in us** when going through life. If you take a second to see the thought and recognize that you didn't actually consciously think it, a space opens up for you to think differently than your automatic self.

Realize that your initial reaction or approach can always be altered for the better. Accept the thoughts that initially come up throughout life but then **actively choose what actions you want to take.**

"Man is free at the moment he wishes to be." - Voltaire

Night 46

TONIGHT I'LL SLEEP AT: _____ & TOMORROW I'LL WAKE UP AT: _____

✏️ OPENING UP ABOUT MY DAY:

_____
_____
_____
_____
_____
_____
_____

☀️ MY MORNING RITUAL TOMORROW WILL BE: *Completed?*

1. _____ ☐
2. _____ ☐
3. _____ ☐
4. _____ ☐
5. _____ ☐

Day 47

LAST NIGHT I SLEPT AT: _____ & WOKE UP TODAY AT: _____

🐸 MY MOST IMPORTANT TASK FOR TODAY IS:

_____

🎯 ONE WAY I CAN IMPROVE LIFE BY 1% IS:

_____

Day 48: **Success Story**

Richard Branson - Founder of Virgin Group™; Net Worth $4.8 B

Branson wakes up at 5:45 A.M. on a daily basis, even when staying at his private island, leaving the curtains drawn so the sun gets him up. The entrepreneur even has a "Why I Wake Up Early" blog. Branson spends his mornings doing physical activity to get his energy levels up and feel his endorphins kick in with either kitesurfing, swimming or tennis.

"I have always been an early riser. Like keeping a positive outlook or keeping fit, waking up early is a habit which you must work on to maintain. Over my 50 years in business I have learned that if I rise early I can achieve so much more in a day and therefore in life.... By rising early I'm able to do some exercise and spend time with my family, which puts me in a great mind frame before getting down to business." - Richard Branson

Branson says that working out gives him at least four additional hours of productive time every day.

Consider adding exercising to your morning routine if you haven't already.

"One key to success is to have lunch at the time of day most people have breakfast." - Robert Brault

Night 47

TONIGHT I'LL SLEEP AT: _____ & TOMORROW I'LL WAKE UP AT: _____

✏️ OPENING UP ABOUT MY DAY:

_____
_____
_____
_____
_____
_____

☀️ MY MORNING RITUAL TOMORROW WILL BE: *Completed?*

(3-day challenge idea: review 1 chapter of a beloved old book).

1. _____ ☐
2. _____ ☐
3. _____ ☐
4. _____ ☐
5. _____ ☐

Day 48

LAST NIGHT I SLEPT AT: _____ & WOKE UP TODAY AT: _____

🐎 MY MOST IMPORTANT TASK FOR TODAY IS:

_____

⏲️ ONE WAY I CAN IMPROVE LIFE BY 1% IS:

_____

Day 49: **YouTube Alert!**

Name: <u>FitLife.Tv with Drew Canole</u>   536,000+ SUBSCRIBERS ▶

Drew's story is a very inspiring one. He went from being ~20% body fat to less than 7%! He lives a happy, healthy lifestyle and is great at providing actionable guidance for you to follow.

Drew has done a lot of research on nutrition and is a huge proponent of using vegetable juicing to cut fat and increase the amount of micronutrients your body is getting.

Although his channel's main focus does not just line up with only building a healthy morning, his channel is a great starting point for anybody looking to take their nutrition to the next level, to cut fat, pack on muscle, and overall increase their body's health & happiness every day!

Recommend video to search on YouTube: 7 Step Morning Ritual with Drew Canole
Subscribe here: www.youtube.com/user/fitlifetv

"In the morning a man walks with his whole body; in the evening, just with his legs." - Ralph Waldo Emerson

Night 48

TONIGHT I'LL SLEEP AT: _____ & TOMORROW I'LL WAKE UP AT: _____

✏️ OPENING UP ABOUT MY DAY:

_____
_____
_____
_____
_____
_____
_____

☀️ MY MORNING RITUAL TOMORROW WILL BE: *Completed?*

1. _____ ☐
2. _____ ☐
3. _____ ☐
4. _____ ☐
5. _____ ☐

Day 49

LAST NIGHT I SLEPT AT: _____ & WOKE UP TODAY AT: _____

🐸 MY MOST IMPORTANT TASK FOR TODAY IS:

_____

🎯 ONE WAY I CAN IMPROVE LIFE BY 1% IS:

_____

Day 50: **Pro-Tip**

<u>Wait until you finish your morning ritual before using your phone.</u>

Bathe, get dressed and groom before you switch on your smart phone (or take it out of airplane mode). You'll be fully ready to tackle the day ahead versus sitting around in your pajamas and bathrobe fiddling with your phone. Not only does it help you avoid wasting the extremely valuable morning hours, but you'll notice just how correlated stress is with your phone. This is because your phone is really your outlet to the world. Your outlet to work, to social media, and there's a lot of anxiety that comes with those outlets.

Try as long as possible to avoid messing around with your phone until you absolutely need to use it when your day has started. It'll do you wonders!

Going in airplane mode when you go to sleep and leaving your phone off until you complete your morning ritual will set you up for success here.

"Every morning in Africa, a Gazelle wakes up. It knows it must run faster than the fastest lion or it will be killed. Every morning a Lion wakes up. It knows it must outrun the slowest Gazelle or it will starve to death. It doesn't matter whether you are a Lion or a Gazelle... when the sun comes up, you'd better be running." - Anonymous

Night 49

TONIGHT I'LL SLEEP AT: _____ & TOMORROW I'LL WAKE UP AT: _____

✏️ OPENING UP ABOUT MY DAY:

_____
_____
_____
_____
_____
_____

☀️ MY MORNING RITUAL TOMORROW WILL BE: *Completed?*

1. _____ ☐
2. _____ ☐
3. _____ ☐
4. _____ ☐
5. _____ ☐

Day 50

LAST NIGHT I SLEPT AT: _____ & WOKE UP TODAY AT: _____

🐎 MY MOST IMPORTANT TASK FOR TODAY IS:

_____

🧭 ONE WAY I CAN IMPROVE LIFE BY 1% IS:

_____

Day 51: **Favorite Resources**

Dance, party, and jumpstart your day at 6 A.M. at Daybreaker!

Does the sound of a 6 A.M. morning dance party spark any excitement in you?? Well that's what a Daybreaker is— one of the absolute BEST ways to start off your morning.

Daybreaker is truly a one of a kind event. The community there is AMAZING. It's full of love, acceptance, happiness, and dancing. Also, instead of alcohol, they serve healthy snacks and coffee.

They're a relatively new company but are expanding quickly. If they're not in your city you can petition them to move there too.

Check Daybreaker out here: **www.Daybreaker.com**

Fun fact: after Mikey, one of the authors of this journal, missed a Daybreaker event by not being able to wake up early, he set out to change his morning habits. This journal would likely not be in existence if it weren't for Daybreaker!

"Front-loading my day (getting a whole bunch done in the morning) is my productivity secret." – Celeste Headlee

Night 50

TONIGHT I'LL SLEEP AT: _____ & TOMORROW I'LL WAKE UP AT: _____

✏️ OPENING UP ABOUT MY DAY:

_____
_____
_____
_____
_____
_____
_____

☀ MY MORNING RITUAL TOMORROW WILL BE: *Completed?*

1. _____ ☐
2. _____ ☐
3. _____ ☐
4. _____ ☐
5. _____ ☐

Day 51

LAST NIGHT I SLEPT AT: _____ & WOKE UP TODAY AT: _____

🐸 MY MOST IMPORTANT TASK FOR TODAY IS:

_____

⏱ ONE WAY I CAN IMPROVE LIFE BY 1% IS:

_____

Day 52: Affirmations

1. Find a quiet area where you can do this in private so you can be at ease. If you can't find a private space, say these in your head while pretending you're screaming them from a mountaintop.

2. Think of a time when you felt absolutely powerful - **when you felt on top of the world**. Tap into every emotion you had at that moment and get yourself into that state right now. How were you feeling then - Powerful? Unstoppable? Strong? Incredible!? Get into it now!!!!

3. Now feel your intensity grow tenfold! Say this with deep passion:

I am noticing that waking up early is requiring less and less effort. I am turning into someone who immediately wakes up as soon as my alarm goes off. I will take full advantage of every day by waking up early.

I must minimize my distractions at night, disconnect from time-sucking applications and unfulfilling entertainment, and I will move head-first to achieving incredible clarity and success in my life!

Repeat this **one more time.**

I WILL ACCOMPLISH IMPORTANT AND NECESSARY TASKS TODAY BECAUSE I AM FOCUSED AND ENERGIZED FROM MY MORNING RITUAL

"The way I define happiness is being the creator of your experience, choosing to take pleasure in what you have, right now, regardless of the circumstances, while being the best you that you can be." - Leo Babauta

Night 51

TONIGHT I'LL SLEEP AT: _____ & TOMORROW I'LL WAKE UP AT: _____

✏️ OPENING UP ABOUT MY DAY:

_____
_____
_____
_____
_____
_____
_____

☀️ MY MORNING RITUAL TOMORROW WILL BE: *Completed?*

1. _____ ☐
2. _____ ☐
3. _____ ☐
4. _____ ☐
5. _____ ☐

Day 52

LAST NIGHT I SLEPT AT: _____ & WOKE UP TODAY AT: _____

🐸 MY MOST IMPORTANT TASK FOR TODAY IS:

_____

🎯 ONE WAY I CAN IMPROVE LIFE BY 1% IS:

_____

Day 53: **Daily Challenge**

Regardless of your mood or energy levels in the mornings, let your actions set the tone for your day.

Although some morning people wake up full of energy and ready to start their day every day… the majority wake up *just as tired* as everybody else. But the ones who really conquer their mornings are the ones who take massive action to fill their bodies up with energy throughout that phase of being tired. These are the people who literally create energy within their bodies by forcing themselves to move quickly and powerfully.

Your body's energy levels are much harder to change through mental battles (i.e. trying to motivate yourself to get out of bed) versus **taking action** (i.e. forcing yourself to jump out of bed and MOVE!)

In summary:
- Your mindset changes from your actions.
- Your actions are what you always have control over (while you can't control the thoughts that come through your head).
- So take the right actions to succeed regardless of your emotional state… your emotions will be set by the actions you take.

"Life is too short," she panicked. "I want more." He nodded slowly. "Wake up earlier."- Dr. SunWolf

Night 52

TONIGHT I'LL SLEEP AT: _____ & TOMORROW I'LL WAKE UP AT: _____

✎ OPENING UP ABOUT MY DAY:

_____
_____
_____
_____
_____
_____
_____

☀ MY MORNING RITUAL TOMORROW WILL BE: *Completed?*

1. _____ ☐
2. _____ ☐
3. _____ ☐
4. _____ ☐
5. _____ ☐

Day 53

LAST NIGHT I SLEPT AT: _____ & WOKE UP TODAY AT: _____

🐸 MY MOST IMPORTANT TASK FOR TODAY IS:

_____

⊕ ONE WAY I CAN IMPROVE LIFE BY 1% IS:

_____

Day 54: **Pro-Tip**

<u>Jumpstart your day by taking a cold shower.</u>

Cold showers are one of the greatest tests of discipline out there. And once you conquer them, you feel ***unstoppable***.

Cold showers accomplish the following
1. Floods your body with health benefits (amazing for your cardiovascular system)
2. Physically shocks your body to wake up and feel full of energy. This is incredibly useful for turbocharging your mornings
3. Makes you feel like a mental warrior who can conquer anything
4. Trains your discipline which carries into building other habits

A great approach is to ease into cold showers. Start hot and each shower make it about 2-5% colder. As time goes on it's very common to genuinely prefer cold showers to hot ones, or at least a mix of both. Ending with cold for 30 seconds is best.

Double Pro-Tip: Getting a waterproof shower speaker makes this process a lot more enjoyable too (dancing through the cold is VERY effective). They're fairly inexpensive on Amazon.

"Don't underestimate the power of thoughts and words. What you tell yourself every morning will set your mind and life on that path. Talk success, victory, happiness and blessings over your destiny."
– Nina Bolivares

Night 53

TONIGHT I'LL SLEEP AT: _____ & TOMORROW I'LL WAKE UP AT: _____

✏️ OPENING UP ABOUT MY DAY:

_____
_____
_____
_____
_____
_____

(3-day challenge idea: walk 2 blocks while listening to a podcast).

☀ MY MORNING RITUAL TOMORROW WILL BE:

Completed?

1. _____ ☐
2. _____ ☐
3. _____ ☐
4. _____ ☐
5. _____ ☐

Day 54

LAST NIGHT I SLEPT AT: _____ & WOKE UP TODAY AT: _____

🐸 MY MOST IMPORTANT TASK FOR TODAY IS:

_____

⏰ ONE WAY I CAN IMPROVE LIFE BY 1% IS:

_____

Day 55: **Success Story**

<u>**Ursula Burns, Xerox™ CEO. Reported Compensation in 2014: $18.8 Million.**</u>

Ursula was raised in the rough and tumble public housing projects on the Lower East Side of Manhattan. She was told by many people that she had three strikes against her: She was black. She was a girl. And she was poor.

Burns started as an intern at Xerox; *she's now the CEO*. Her story is an incredible one and she used her mornings to elevate her life and career.

She uses this time to stay in shape, scheduling an hour of personal training at 6:00 A.M. twice a week. Certain days she's known to work from 5:15 A.M. sometimes until midnight. It's no wonder she's become incredibly successful in her life.

"I have always been delighted at the prospect of a new day, a fresh try, one more start, with perhaps a bit of magic waiting somewhere behind the morning." - B. Priestley

Night 54

TONIGHT I'LL SLEEP AT: _____ & TOMORROW I'LL WAKE UP AT: _____

✎ OPENING UP ABOUT MY DAY:

_____
_____
_____
_____
_____
_____

☀ MY MORNING RITUAL TOMORROW WILL BE: *Completed?*

1. _____ ☐
2. _____ ☐
3. _____ ☐
4. _____ ☐
5. _____ ☐

Day 55

LAST NIGHT I SLEPT AT: _____ & WOKE UP TODAY AT: _____

🐸 MY MOST IMPORTANT TASK FOR TODAY IS:

_____

⊕ ONE WAY I CAN IMPROVE LIFE BY 1% IS:

_____

Day 56: **Daily Challenge**

Challenge: Write down your morning routine from least difficult to most difficult activities & do them in that order.

A very good practice is to think about all of the things that absolutely must get done in a day and work them into chains. Unless the order actually matters, the easiest habits should be loaded up front, and the most difficult ones should be left for last.

This ensures that you maximize the benefit of momentum as you move through your chain. Every small victory you win by moving through the chain gives you the power to finish it off strongly. The sequence of easiest activities to most difficult will provide you with a sense of satisfaction and confidence that you can build on.

It's through this process that habits give you freedom – chains take care of the necessities of life and leave you with time and willpower to make forward progress.

"Giving myself time, care, and attention in the morning has been crucial to significantly reducing my stress levels and consistently increasing my capacity to perform, have clarity, and take action."
– Aiste Gazdar

Night 55

TONIGHT I'LL SLEEP AT: _____ & TOMORROW I'LL WAKE UP AT: _____

✏️ OPENING UP ABOUT MY DAY:

_____
_____
_____
_____
_____
_____
_____

☀️ MY MORNING RITUAL TOMORROW WILL BE: *Completed?*

1. _____ ☐
2. _____ ☐
3. _____ ☐
4. _____ ☐
5. _____ ☐

Day 56

LAST NIGHT I SLEPT AT: _____ & WOKE UP TODAY AT: _____

🐸 MY MOST IMPORTANT TASK FOR TODAY IS:

_____

🧭 ONE WAY I CAN IMPROVE LIFE BY 1% IS:

_____

Day 57: **Pro-Tip**

<u>*Eat healthy - smaller decisions have chain effects on your day.*</u>

Decisions like what kind of food you eat, whether you start a difficult task or procrastinate, or whether you clarify an internal stress or let it go unnoticed, all have compounding effects way into your life's future.

Very commonly, yet unknowingly, these smaller decisions lead to a chain of effects that will negatively effect us. A heavy meal will lead to feeling slow and unproductive. This will lead to poor leadership and decision making. This will cause problems that need precious time to get fixed and important work to go unfinished. Chances are this will lead to stress, guilt, which will thus lead to making poor decisions once again that will continue the cycle.

Keep this chain of effects in mind when making smaller decisions throughout your day - remember the implications go way farther than just now. A poor decision now is practically equivalent to shooting your future self in the foot just hours ahead.

"Laugh and the world laughs with you; snore, and you sleep alone!"
- Anthony Burgess

Night 56

TONIGHT I'LL SLEEP AT: _____ & TOMORROW I'LL WAKE UP AT: _____

✏️ OPENING UP ABOUT MY DAY:

_____
_____
_____
_____
_____
_____

☀️ MY MORNING RITUAL TOMORROW WILL BE: *Completed?*

1. _____ ☐
2. _____ ☐
3. _____ ☐
4. _____ ☐
5. _____ ☐

Day 57

LAST NIGHT I SLEPT AT: _____ & WOKE UP TODAY AT: _____

🐎 MY MOST IMPORTANT TASK FOR TODAY IS:

_____

⏱ ONE WAY I CAN IMPROVE LIFE BY 1% IS:

_____

Day 58: **YouTube Alert!**

Name: **_Robin Sharma._** 348,000+ SUBSCRIBERS ▶

Robin Sharma is a well-known best selling author and speaker who has dedicated his life to helping people transform their lives in personal and professional settings. He's authored 15 global best-sellers and he's an absolute expert on leadership. He has a lot of insight to give to the world. Check out the link below about waking up early and see what other pieces of treasure you can find in his videos!

Some topics he covers: Waking up early, meditation, increasing willpower, beating procrastination, genuinely living happily every day.

Search this video on YouTube: **Robin Sharma on "How to Wake Up Early"**
Subscribe for free here: **www.youtube.com/user/sharmaleadership**

"The secret of your future is hidden in your daily routine."
- Mike Murdock

Night 57

TONIGHT I'LL SLEEP AT: _____ & TOMORROW I'LL WAKE UP AT: _____

✏️ OPENING UP ABOUT MY DAY:

_____
_____
_____
_____
_____
_____
_____

☀ MY MORNING RITUAL TOMORROW WILL BE: *Completed?*

1. _____ ☐
2. _____ ☐
3. _____ ☐
4. _____ ☐
5. _____ ☐

Day 58

LAST NIGHT I SLEPT AT: _____ & WOKE UP TODAY AT: _____

🐎 MY MOST IMPORTANT TASK FOR TODAY IS:

_____

⬆ ONE WAY I CAN IMPROVE LIFE BY 1% IS:

_____

Day 59: **Success Story**
Oprah Winfrey, founder of OWN. Net Worth: $3.1B

Oprah, the queen herself, is a big proponent of using mornings to start your day off incredibly powerfully.

She wakes up between 6:02am and 6:20am without an alarm (she sets the number in her head each night before! Wow). She makes a cappuccino then works out with the elliptical machine and treadmill.

What sticks out the most is she makes sure to meditate each morning. **Even when she's in a rush, she prioritizes** it and does at least 10 minutes (though usually she aims for 20). She even has a specific meditation room in her house to help with this.

If she's not tapping into things she's grateful for in the morning, she has loads of gratitude journals at night she uses. She was actually a big inspiration for us in creating our next gratitude project called The Greatest Gift.

Have you considered how you could use meditation, or gratitude (or both), in your morning routine?

"Life isn't about finding yourself. Life is about creating yourself."
- George Bernard Shaw

Night 58

TONIGHT I'LL SLEEP AT: _____ & TOMORROW I'LL WAKE UP AT: _____

✏️ OPENING UP ABOUT MY DAY:

_____
_____
_____
_____
_____
_____

☀️ MY MORNING RITUAL TOMORROW WILL BE: *Completed?*

(3-day challenge idea: watch a TED talk each morning).

1. _____ ☐
2. _____ ☐
3. _____ ☐
4. _____ ☐
5. _____ ☐

Day 59

LAST NIGHT I SLEPT AT: _____ & WOKE UP TODAY AT: _____

🐸 MY MOST IMPORTANT TASK FOR TODAY IS:

_____

⏱️ ONE WAY I CAN IMPROVE LIFE BY 1% IS:

_____

Day 60: **Pro-Tip**

<u>Order a new Sidekick Journal to continue mastering your life's habits.</u>

Heads up: you're on the final pages of this journal!

If you're one of the few warriors/warrior princesses who's made it this far, don't lose momentum now. You're entering the time where you can consistently reap the benefits of building up habits.

As of Fall 2018, we offer a series of different Sidekick Journals for different habits you can engrain in yourself. These are:

- The Morning Sidekick Journal
- The Fat Loss & Nutrition Sidekick Journal
- The Meditation Sidekick Journal
- The Greatest Gift (Our all-in-one gratitude journal)

Note: get a sneak peek of these on page 183 of this journal.

We truly hope we've provided enough value to you with this journal that you'd consider ordering another again from us. If not, that's definitely okay, but if you do — you can message us for a special discount code you can use for your order :) - smile@habitnest.com.

"With the new day comes new strength and new thoughts."
— Eleanor Roosevelt

Night 59

TONIGHT I'LL SLEEP AT: _____ & TOMORROW I'LL WAKE UP AT: _____

✏ OPENING UP ABOUT MY DAY:

_____
_____
_____
_____
_____
_____
_____

☀ MY MORNING RITUAL TOMORROW WILL BE: *Completed?*

1. _____ ☐
2. _____ ☐
3. _____ ☐
4. _____ ☐
5. _____ ☐

Day 60

LAST NIGHT I SLEPT AT: _____ & WOKE UP TODAY AT: _____

🐸 MY MOST IMPORTANT TASK FOR TODAY IS:

_____

⊕ ONE WAY I CAN IMPROVE LIFE BY 1% IS:

_____

Day 61: **Affirmations**

1. Find a quiet area where you can do this in private so you can be at ease. If you can't find a private space, say these in your head while pretending you're screaming them from a mountaintop.

2. Think of a time when you felt absolutely powerful - **when you felt on top of the world**. Tap into every emotion you had at that moment and get yourself into that state right now. How were you feeling then - Powerful? Unstoppable? Strong? Incredible!? Get into it now!!!!

3. Now feel your intensity grow tenfold! Say this with deep passion:

Consistently doing my morning routine sparks newfound energy levels and work ethic inside me every day. It skyrockets me on my path to becoming the best version of myself.

By becoming the best version of myself, I am able to spread more love to my friends, family, and everybody around me. I am the leading force behind an ever-growing beacon of positivity in the world!

Repeat this **one more time.**

"Life begins at the end of your comfort zone." – Neale Donald Walsh

Night 60

TONIGHT I'LL SLEEP AT: _____ & TOMORROW I'LL WAKE UP AT: _____

✏️ OPENING UP ABOUT MY DAY:

_____
_____
_____
_____
_____
_____
_____

☀️ MY MORNING RITUAL TOMORROW WILL BE: *Completed?*

1. _____ ☐
2. _____ ☐
3. _____ ☐
4. _____ ☐
5. _____ ☐

Day 61

LAST NIGHT I SLEPT AT: _____ & WOKE UP TODAY AT: _____

🐎 MY MOST IMPORTANT TASK FOR TODAY IS:

_____

⊕ ONE WAY I CAN IMPROVE LIFE BY 1% IS:

_____

Day 62: **Pro-Tip**

Smile at yourself in the mirror for 30 seconds.

This is a can't-miss way to boost your self esteem. Once you get into the habit you'll wonder how you ever got along without it.

Make sure you're smiling; it doesn't have to be a big goofy grin, just the hint of a smile works. This works on a number of different levels, but at the core is the ability it gives you to establish a positive, love-filled relationship with yourself before the day starts.

It's not easy to try this exercise even once and not feel a little bit crazy.

That being said, this one is incredibly effective. The exercise of literally smiling in front of a mirror has been linked to squandering depression and melting away the stresses that secretly build up in us.

What you're doing here is basically checking in with your mind and body on the deepest level. By giving yourself a deep physiological message that you are happy, you force your body to adapt. And daily happiness in 30 seconds can go a long ways.

"Every morning brings new potential, but if you tend to dwell on the misfortunes of the day before, you tend to overlook tremendous opportunities." - Harvey Mackay

Night 61

TONIGHT I'LL SLEEP AT: _____ & TOMORROW I'LL WAKE UP AT: _____

✏️ OPENING UP ABOUT MY DAY:

_____
_____
_____
_____
_____
_____

☀️ MY MORNING RITUAL TOMORROW WILL BE: *Completed?*

1. _____ ☐
2. _____ ☐
3. _____ ☐
4. _____ ☐
5. _____ ☐

Day 62

LAST NIGHT I SLEPT AT: _____ & WOKE UP TODAY AT: _____

🐸 MY MOST IMPORTANT TASK FOR TODAY IS:

_____

🎯 ONE WAY I CAN IMPROVE LIFE BY 1% IS:

_____

Day 63: **Affirmations**

1. Find a quiet area where you can do this in private so you can be at ease. If you can't find a private space, say these in your head while pretending you're screaming them from a mountaintop.

2. Think of a time when you felt absolutely powerful - **when you felt on top of the world**. Tap into every emotion you had at that moment and get yourself into that state right now. How were you feeling then - Powerful? Unstoppable? Strong? Incredible!? Get into it now!!!!

3. Now feel your intensity grow tenfold! Say this with deep passion:

---

*Day after day I am realizing that my potential in life is **absolutely limitless**. I am an unstoppable force for good.*

I am going to destroy every obstacle and challenge that comes in my path because I know that nothing is bigger than me.

By improving myself every day, day after day after day, I am creating a snowball effect that will propel me through life to incredible success.

Repeat this **one more time.**

Night 62

TONIGHT I'LL SLEEP AT: _____ & TOMORROW I'LL WAKE UP AT: _____

✏ OPENING UP ABOUT MY DAY:

_____
_____
_____
_____
_____
_____

☀ MY MORNING RITUAL TOMORROW WILL BE: *Completed?*

1. _____ ☐
2. _____ ☐
3. _____ ☐
4. _____ ☐
5. _____ ☐

Day 63

LAST NIGHT I SLEPT AT: _____ & WOKE UP TODAY AT: _____

🐸 MY MOST IMPORTANT TASK FOR TODAY IS:

_____

⏱ ONE WAY I CAN IMPROVE LIFE BY 1% IS:

_____

Day 64: **Pro-Tip**

The next time you feel "out of it," take physical action (not mental) to shift your body's state.

Preparing for your off days and days of struggle is absolutely critical. It's what many of the Pro-Tips in this book cover. Shifting your off days to work in your favor is what's most challenging yet the most rewarding.

Let's be real - having an off day is inevitable and you will absolutely hit another point where you feel like total crap. Trying to mentally battle yourself to "feel better" won't do you any good in this state.

What IS incredibly effective is taking a **physical action** to shock your body physiologically. The next time you feel out of it, force yourself to take a physical action to shift your body's state (by boosting oxygen, adrenaline, and/or endorphins). Some specific actions you can take the next time you feel out of it are:

1. Take 5 long inhales deep into your stomach.
2. Work out or move around (even for 30 seconds).
3. Take a cold shower (this is for the truly crazy ones out there).

"Early rising not only gives us more life in the same number of years, but adds, likewise, to their number; and not only enables us to enjoy more of existence in the same time, but increases also the measure."
- Caleb C. Colton

Night 63

TONIGHT I'LL SLEEP AT: _____ & TOMORROW I'LL WAKE UP AT: _____

✏️ OPENING UP ABOUT MY DAY:

_____
_____
_____
_____
_____
_____
_____

☀️ MY MORNING RITUAL TOMORROW WILL BE: *Completed?*

1. _____ ☐
2. _____ ☐
3. _____ ☐
4. _____ ☐
5. _____ ☐

Day 64

LAST NIGHT I SLEPT AT: _____ & WOKE UP TODAY AT: _____

🐸 MY MOST IMPORTANT TASK FOR TODAY IS:

_____

⏱️ ONE WAY I CAN IMPROVE LIFE BY 1% IS:

_____

Day 65: **Success Story**

Scott Adams, creator of Dilbert™; Net Worth: $75 million.

Business Insider reported that Adams designs his morning routine to maximize his creativity. Adams was quoted saying, "My value is based on my best ideas in any given day, not the number of hours I work."

Adams has a protein bar and coffee every morning. "I give myself this 'treat' knowing I can be trained like any other animal. And I want to train myself to enjoy waking up and being productive (it totally works)."

Have you considered implementing any morning routines to stimulate creativity for the rest of the day? One that comes to mind is brainstorming out 10 ideas (about anything!) as recommended by author James Altucher.

"My morning routine definitely sets the tone for the rest of my day. If I'm rushed and stressed in the morning, that will carry through my work day."
– Tessa Miller

Night 64

TONIGHT I'LL SLEEP AT: _____ & TOMORROW I'LL WAKE UP AT: _____

✏ OPENING UP ABOUT MY DAY:

_____
_____
_____
_____
_____
_____
_____

☀ MY MORNING RITUAL TOMORROW WILL BE: *Completed?*

1. _____ ☐
2. _____ ☐
3. _____ ☐
4. _____ ☐
5. _____ ☐

Day 65

LAST NIGHT I SLEPT AT: _____ & WOKE UP TODAY AT: _____

🐂 MY MOST IMPORTANT TASK FOR TODAY IS:

_____

🎯 ONE WAY I CAN IMPROVE LIFE BY 1% IS:

_____

Phase 3 Medal Earned!

Day 66: **Congratulations!!!** 🥂

You've made it to the end of the journal. **You now OWN your mornings,** one of the most difficult habits to master in your life.

For you to have gotten this far means you've earned a very serious congratulations. You need to celebrate because your willpower and confidence should be soaring through the roof. You've gained lessons about yourself not many dare to approach. You've struggled with your own mind, body and heart and gained some serious control over them. You fully understand that you have the power in you to accomplish ANY goal you put your mind to.

This is a skill you've built inside you that you can turn on whenever you need it at any future point in your lifetime. **That's so awesome.**

You are a WARRIOR and we (Amir, Ariel, & Mikey) hope you continue to build on your habit success and personal development for the rest of your life.

Note: We constantly (daily!) read reviews for all of our products on Amazon. It would mean the absolute world if you could leave us a genuine review of the journal there.

PS we're always aiming for 5/5 satisfaction, so if anything is off you can always email us directly at smile@habitnest.com first so we can take care of you!

Night 65

TONIGHT I'LL SLEEP AT: _____ & TOMORROW I'LL WAKE UP AT: _____

✏️ OPENING UP ABOUT MY DAY:

_____
_____
_____
_____
_____
_____
_____

☀️ MY MORNING RITUAL TOMORROW WILL BE: *Completed?*

1. _____ ☐
2. _____ ☐
3. _____ ☐
4. _____ ☐
5. _____ ☐

Day 66

LAST NIGHT I SLEPT AT: _____ & WOKE UP TODAY AT: _____

🐎 MY MOST IMPORTANT TASK FOR TODAY IS:

_____

⊕ ONE WAY I CAN IMPROVE LIFE BY 1% IS:

_____

~~PHASE 3.~~

MASTERED.

Phase 3 Recap: Days 22-66+

1. Think about what your life looked like before you began this habit — what are you doing differently now? How do you feel?

_____
_____
_____
_____

2. What unforeseen effects has your life gained from all this?

_____
_____
_____
_____

3. When you are struggling with this habit in the future, what are the key factors you should remember to do again?

_____
_____
_____

4. What daily tracking and accountability can you have going forward to maintain the momentum you've built here?

_____
_____

- *Fin* -

So... What Now?

Although you should feel very accomplished for getting through this entire journal... know that you built this habit to *continually improve your life. Don't stop now. This is only the beginning.*

One huge factor to this is tracking your progress. Once you stop tracking, it makes it exponentially easier for you to skip having a productive morning (due to the lack of accountability with yourself).

Remember: **Every single day in your life where you start your morning with focus, intent, and energy will automatically be a better day of your life.**

You only stand to gain from continuing this habit.

Meet The Habit Nest Team

Amir Atighehchi graduated from USC's Marshall School of Business in 2013. He began to study the behaviors of the world's most successful people. This catapulted him to start building many "success-habits" into his daily routine. He's a big believer in BJ Fogg's Tiny Habits™ model and applies it to every new habit he forms. Mikey and Amir are also co-founders of the bicycle lock company, Nutlock.

Mikey Ahdoot transformed his life from a 200+ pound, video game addict to someone who was doing 17 daily habits consistently at one point. From ice cold showers to brainstorming 10 ideas a day (shoutout to James Altucher) to celebrating life every damn day, he first hand is becoming a habit routine machine that sets himself up for success daily. He is a graduate of USC's Marshall School of Business and proud trojan.

Ari Banayan began studying habits and their relation to success when he was seventeen. Through experimenting with different lifestyle habits, he quickly learned how important it is to take care of ourselves mentally, physically and emotionally to operate at maximum capacity. Ariel graduated at the top of his class from the University of Southern California Gould School of Law in 2016.

What Life Changing Habit Will YOU Conquer Next?

The Greatest Gift helps you build the incredible habit of gratitude… and give a gift of pure love at the same time.

It's a gratitude journal you fill out with 21 stories for **one specific person** of how they've impacted your life and how you're thankful for them.

When you're finished, you **surprise them** with the finished journal as a gift.

We help you tell your story with:
- **30 story ideas** to spark what to write about
- **Specific guidance** on how to tell your story
- Journal + box + card + envelope + ribbon + wrapping paper to make the **perfect presentation they'll remember FOREVER**

Skyrocket your positivity and appreciation for the world, all while giving a heartfelt gift of gratitude to someone you love.

Get yours at: **greatestgift.io**

Meditation Sidekick
Journal

This journal is built to help two types of people:

1. To help **newcomers or past strugglers** to easily own the practice of meditation.

2. To help **constant meditators** push their practice to another level.

Layout of the journal

1. **Building the foundation** - get a quick insight into the *science behind meditation* and get an idea of what you're likely to experience during it.

2. **Accountability** - track your practice daily to see your progress and hold yourself accountable in staying consistent.

3. **Learn in bite-sized chunks** - get daily exposure to different types of meditations (i.e. transcendental, gratitude, physical body, etc.) and see which ones impact your life the most.

One thing we love: The journal is not just designed to help you meditate effectively, but more importantly, to **help you reach the end goal of consistently living mindfully every day.**

Get yours at SidekickJournal.com/meditation

Sample Journal Page

DATE

 TODAY I WILL MEDITATE AT: **FOR AT LEAST:**

7:30 a.m. ✓   5 minutes ✓

 ONE UPCOMING MENTAL OR EMOTIONAL HURDLE TO BE MINDFUL OF:

My presentation for my boss at work – own it!

✓ **BENEFITS I FELT TODAY (CIRCLE):**

Feel Happier · More Creative · Increased Willpower · Improved Focus · More Energized · Reduced Stress

 WHAT DOES MY INTERNAL DIALOGUE CONSIST OF?

I realize that I think about my appearance A LOT... and I immediately assume people judge me for it.

 ONE SMALL WAY I CAN IMPROVE MY INTERNAL DIALOGUE:

I could be more understanding when I'm feeling self-conscious and willingly accept myself for how I look.

OPENING UP ABOUT MY DAY:

Today was a rollercoaster. I realize that when I'm working with others, I prefer not to rely on them to get things done. It's something I want to work on improving because I make myself feel anxious when it happens.

Fat Loss & Nutrition Sidekick
Journal

This journal has a similar layout to the Morning Sidekick Journal. It's designed to be flexible and adaptable to whatever food goals you may have. Early testers have successfully used it to implement:

- Calorie counting
- Fat loss and/or muscle building
- General healthy eating
- Paleo / vegan / IIFYM / ketosis / other custom diets

The journal serves as your personal trainer for losing weight and **regaining control over your eating habits** quickly and effectively.

It allows you to **perfectly track** all that you need for YOUR body's optimum nutrition and fat loss. These include:

- Daily caloric intake goal
- Water drinking goal
- Exercise goal
- Planned vs. actual meals, (& caloric intake for each)
- Snacks, alcohol, and other intake
- Upcoming big meals to watch out for

One thing we love: A lot of the tips are designed to help you **break the association** that may exist between **your confidence / happiness** and **your body weight.**

Get yours at SidekickJournal.com/nutrition

Sample Journal Page

A 100-200 calorie range works well!

TODAY'S CALORIE GOAL

1,900 - 2,100 ✓

DATE

💧 **WATER DRINKING GOAL**

Two 500mL bottles ✓

🚶 **EXERCISE GOAL**

2 mile jog ☐

🍽 **TODAY'S MEALS**

#	📅 Planned	✓ Actual	Calories Eaten?
1.	3 eggs w/ 2 rice cakes	3 eggs w/ 2 rice cakes	340
2.	Chicken + Broccoli + cauliflower	Burrito (tortilla, avocado, tomatoes, chicken)	800
3.	Salmon w/ asparagus	Salmon w/ asparagus	500
4.	....	....	....
5.	....	....	....

(optional)

🍎 **SNACKS, DRINKS, & OTHER**

30 almonds	210
One snickerdoodle cookie	250

TODAY'S TOTAL: 2,100

🏃 **POTENTIAL FOOD OBSTACLE(S) TO LOOK OUT FOR TOMORROW:**

Resist the cookies at lunch!

⬆ **ONE WAY I CAN IMPROVE BY 1% TOMORROW IS:**

If I bring a snack to work, I can eat that instead of sweets.

Share the Love

If you're reading this, that means you've come pretty far from where you were 2 months ago. You should be extremely proud of yourself!

If you believe this journal has had a positive impact on your life, we invite you to consider gifting a new one to a friend.

Is there a holiday coming up? Is there a special birthday around the corner? Or do you just want to put a smile on someone's face and do something incredible for them?

Gifting this journal is the absolute best way to show any gratitude you may have for what we've written here, as well as serving as a force of good through giving back to others. And you can rest assured that you're helping improve another person's life at the same time.

We created a discount code for getting this far that can be used for any Morning Sidekick Journal reorder (make sure to use the same email address you placed the order with).

If you decide to, feel free to re-order here:
www.SidekickJournal.com

Use code **MorningChamp15** for 15% off!

Content Index

Day 1: Pro-Tip……….Your morning ritual starts the night before

Day 2: Daily Challenge…………….Use off-days to rewire your brain

Day 3: Pro-Tip……..…………...Condition yourself week-by-week

Day 4: Daily Challenge………Write down what impedes your success

Day 5: Pro-Tip…..…………….Find a morning accountability buddy

Day 6: Pro-Tip……………… Some strategies for chronic snoozers

Day 7: Affirmations……..…………...……………Affirmation #1

Day 8: Daily Challenge……….Pay attention your daily mini-decisions

Day 9: Super Read………………...*The Miracle Morning* by Hal Elrod

Day 10: Pro-Tip…..……………………..Reboot your sleep schedule

Day 11: Affirmations……………………………...…Affirmation #2

Day 12: Success Story………………..……………Arianna Huffington

Day 13: Double Pro-Tip…………...……Drink ice water and blast music

Day 14: Favorite Podcasts…..……...……...Sleep With Me Podcast

Day 15: Daily Challenge……….Pick an activity you'll be excited about

Day 16: Affirmations……………..……………………Affirmation #3

Day 17: Pro-Tip…………………………….Become a ninja napper

Day 18: Favorite Podcasts…………………….The 5am Miracle Podcast

Day 18: Favorite Podcasts......................The 5am Miracle Podcast

Day 19: Pro-Tip.........................Use grayscale mode on your phone

Day 20: Affirmations...Affirmation #4

Day 21: Success Story..Benjamin Franklin

Day 22: Pro-Tip................................Get to know your body clock

Day 23: Daily Challenge......Take one action out of your comfort zone

Day 24: Affirmations...Affirmation #5

Day 25: Super Read............................*Wake Up Successful* by SJ Scott

Day 26: Daily Challenge............................Maintain consistency

Day 27: Favorite Podcasts.........Smart Passive Income with Pat Flynn

Day 28: Affirmations...Affirmation #6

Day 29: Favorite Resources............Sleep Cycle™ (phone application)

Day 30: Success Story..Gerry Laybourne

Day 31: Affirmation..Affirmation #7

Day 32: Pro-Tip.................Write down your desired wake up time

Day 33: Daily Challenge..............Shift between "off" and "on" days

Day 34: Success Story...Bob Iger

Day 35: Affirmations...Affirmation #8

Day 36: Success Story...John Paul DeJoria

Day 37: Daily Challenge.............Remove your images of perfection

Day 38: Favorite Podcast......MorningCoach.com with JB Glossinger

Day 39: Pro-Tip.........................Keep your phone out of reach

Day 40: Daily Challenge........Think about actions today vs. tomorrow

Day 41: Pro-Tip.....................Don't check e-mail in the mornings

Day 42: Favorite Podcasts.........................The Tim Ferriss Show

Day 43: Affirmations...Affirmation #9

Day 44: Pro-Tip + Affirmation...................Set your morning's intent

Day 45: Pro-Tip........................Set your "lights out" time early on

Day 46: Success Story..Tim Cook

Day 47: Daily Challenge........Discriminate against habitual thoughts

Day 48: Success Story...Richard Branson

Day 49: YouTube Alert!......................FitLife.tv with Drew Canole

Day 50: Pro-Tip.....................Don't use your phone immediately

Day 51: Favorite Tools...............Daybreaker: Morning Dance Party

Day 52: Affirmations...Affirmation #10

Day 53: Daily Challenge............Let your actions set your day's tone

Day 54: Pro-Tip..Take cold showers

Day 55: Success Story..Ursula Burns

Day 56: Daily Challenge..................Do easy morning routines first

Day 57: Pro-Tip..Eat Healthier

Day 58: YouTube Alert!..Robin Sharma

Day 59: Success Story..Oprah Winfrey

Day 60: Pro-Tip..........................Re-order Your Sidekick Journal

Day 61: Affirmations................................... Affirmation #11

Day 62: Pro-Tip.........................Smile at yourself for 30 seconds

Day 63: Affirmations..............................Affirmation #12

Day 64: Pro-Tip..............................Physically change your state

Day 65: Success Story..Scott Adams

Day 66: Congratulations!...........................Mama, I made it

How Was This Journal Created?

We formulated the journal as a mix between what we find personally effective through our own experience as well as through researching published scientific material and books on the newest, most relevant information we could find.

The following is a mix of studies we used to formulate the journal - some points take ideas found in some sources and mix them with our own experience or with other research points.

Some of the main sources of inspiration came from: Kelly McGonigal's *The Willpower Instinct* (a very science-based book on willpower, it's incredible) and Brian Tracy's *Eat That Frog*.

It is a bit difficult to assign specific studies to specific pages in the book as there is a decent amount of overlap in different sections, though we will do our best.

The "Why"

Fishbach, Ayelet, and Ravi Dhar. "Goals as Excuses or Guides: The Liberating Effect of Perceived Goal Progress on Choice." Journal of Consumer Research, vol. 32, no. 3, 2005, pp. 370–377., doi:10.1086/497548.

The "What"

Gardner, Benjamin, et al. "Making Health Habitual: the Psychology of 'Habit-Formation' and General Practice." *British Journal of General Practice*, vol. 62, no. 605, 2012, pp. 664–666., doi:10.3399/bjgp12x659466.

The "How"

Tangney, June P., et al. "High Self-Control Predicts Good Adjustment, Less Pathology, Better Grades, and Interpersonal Success." Journal of Personality, vol. 72, no. 2, 2004, pp. 271–324., doi:10.1111/j.0022-3506.2004.00263.x.

Tracking Pages

Fishbach, Ayelet, and Ravi Dhar. "Goals as Excuses or Guides: The Liberating Effect of Perceived Goal Progress on Choice." Journal of Consumer Research, vol. 32, no. 3, 2005, pp. 370–377., doi:10.1086/497548.

Fogg, BJ. "What Causes Behavior Change?" *BJ Fogg's Behavior Model*, www.behaviormodel.org/index.html.

Daily Content

Dieters cheat: Gailliot, M. T., and R. F. Baumeister. "Self-Regulation and Sexual Restraint: Dispositionally and Temporarily Poor Self-Regulatory Abilities Contribute to Failures at Restraining Sexual Behavior." Personality and Social Psychology Bulletin 33 (2007): 173-86.

Distraction and impulsive choices: Shiv, B., and A. Fedorikhin. "Heart and Mind in Conflict: The Interplay of Affect and Cognition in Consumer Decision Making." Journal of Consumer Research 26 (1999): 278–92. See also Shiv, B., and S. M. Nowlis. "The Effect of Distractions While Tasting a Food Sample: The Interplay of Informational and Affective Components in Subsequent Choice." Journal of Consumer Research 31 (2004): 599–608.

Examples of willpower training programs: Baumeister, R. F., M. Gailliot, C. N. DeWall, and M. Oaten. "Self-Regulation and Personality: How Interventions Increase Regulatory Success, and How Depletion Moderates the Effects of Traits on Behavior." Journal of Personality 74 (2006): 1773–801. See also Muraven, M., R. F. Baumeister, and D. M. Tice. "Longitudinal

Improvement of Self-Regulation through Practice: Building Self-Control Strength through Repeated Exercise." The Journal of Social Psychology 139 (1999): 446–57.

Progress versus commitment: Fishbach, A., and R. Dhar. "Goals as Excuses or Guides: The Liberating Effect of Perceived Goal Progress on Choice." Journal of Consumer Research 32 (2005): 370–77. See also Fishbach, A., R. Dhar, and Y. Zhang. "Subgoals as Substitutes or Complements: The Role of Goal Accessibility." Journal of Personality and Social Psychology 91 (2006): 232–42.

"Recalling Past Temptations: An Information-Processing Perspective on the Dynamics of Self-Control." Journal of Consumer Research 35 (2008): 586–99.

"Practice the Method." The Wim Hof Method - Become Strong, Happy & Healthy, www.wimhofmethod.com/practice-the-method.

Progress versus commitment: Fishbach, A., and R. Dhar. "Goals as Excuses or Guides: The Liberating Effect of Perceived Goal Progress on Choice." Journal of Consumer Research 32 (2005): 370–77. See also Fishbach, A., R. Dhar, and Y. Zhang. "Subgoals as Substitutes or Complements: The Role of Goal Accessibility." Journal of Personality and Social Psychology 91 (2006): 232–42.

The brain gets tired: Inzlicht, M. I., and J. N. Gutsell. "Running on Empty: Neural Signals for Self-Control Failure." Psychological Science 18 (2007): 933–37.

Examples of willpower training programs: Baumeister, R. F., M. Gailliot, C. N. DeWall, and M. Oaten. "Self-Regulation and Personality: How Interventions Increase Regulatory Success, and How Depletion Moderates the Effects of Traits on Behavior." Journal of Personality 74 (2006): 1773–801. See also Muraven, M., R. F. Baumeister, and D. M. Tice. "Longitudinal Improvement of Self-Regulation through Practice: Building Self-Control Strength through Repeated Exercise." The Journal of Social Psychology 139 (1999): 446–57.

Day 23: Daily Challenge.......Take one action out of your comfort zone

Progress versus commitment: Fishbach, A., and R. Dhar. "Goals as Excuses or Guides: The Liberating Effect of Perceived Goal Progress on Choice." Journal of Consumer Research 32 (2005): 370–77. See also Fishbach, A., R. Dhar, and Y. Zhang. "Subgoals as Substitutes or Complements: The Role of Goal Accessibility." Journal of Personality and Social Psychology 91 (2006): 232–42.

Day 26: Daily Challenge.................................Maintain consistency

Examples of willpower training programs: Baumeister, R. F., M. Gailliot, C. N. DeWall, and M. Oaten. "Self-Regulation and Personality: How Interventions Increase Regulatory Success, and How Depletion Moderates the Effects of Traits on Behavior." Journal of Personality 74 (2006): 1773–801. See also Muraven, M., R. F. Baumeister, and D. M. Tice. "Longitudinal Improvement of Self-Regulation through Practice: Building Self-Control Strength through Repeated Exercise." The Journal of Social Psychology 139 (1999): 446–57.

Day 33: Daily Challenge.................Shift between "off" and "on" days

The brain gets tired: Inzlicht, M. I., and J. N. Gutsell. "Running on Empty: Neural Signals for Self-Control Failure." Psychological Science 18 (2007): 933–37.

Dieters cheat: Gailliot, M. T., and R. F. Baumeister. "Self-Regulation and Sexual Restraint: Dispositionally and Temporarily Poor Self-Regulatory Abilities Contribute to Failures at Restraining Sexual Behavior." Personality and Social Psychology Bulletin 33 (2007): 173-86

Day 54: Pro-Tip……………..………...………………..Take cold showers

"Practice the Method." The Wim Hof Method - Become Strong, Happy & Healthy, www.wimhofmethod.com/practice-the-method.